Praise for the Bestselling First Edition

"One of the most brilliant, original, and exciting leadership books I've read in a long time. It will be the most useful and concise book on leadership you'll ever read!"
—Warren Bennis, Distinguished Professor of Business, University of Southern California, and author of *Still Surprised: A Memoir of a Life in Leadership*

"With this compact handbook, Mike Useem provides leaders what they all say they want and need but rarely get: a kick-in-the-pants reminder of those parts of the job they have neglected. The boss is now forewarned."
—Steven Pearlstein, *Washington Post* business columnist and moderator of the On Leadership website

"Leading an enterprise comes down to a set of enduring principles, and *The Leader's Checklist* compellingly captures the most vital. Michael Useem has written *the* essential companion for anybody whose leadership is on the line."
—Ram Charan, advisor to CEOs and boards, and coauthor of the bestsellers *Execution: The Discipline of Getting Things Done* and *The Leadership Pipeline*

"*The Leader's Checklist* reads like an adventure yarn, but packs a goldmine of scholarship and tested observations, that surrounds a list of fifteen principles that guide and teach managers to make on-target, effective business decisions, under real pressure."
—Blogcritics

"*The Leader's Checklist* can refresh a leader's sense of purpose as well as invigorate his or her calling to lead others."
—John Baldoni, SmartBlog on Leadership

"*The Leader's Checklist* gets to the point quickly. It may well set the bar for quality writing and amount of content for other business-related digital books in the future."
—Patricia Faulhaber, Suite101

EXPANDED EDITION

✓ The Leader's Checklist

15 Mission-Critical Principles

Michael Useem

Wharton
DIGITAL PRESS

Philadelphia

Published by Wharton Digital Press

The Wharton School
University of Pennsylvania
3620 Locust Walk
2000 Steinberg Hall-Dietrich Hall
Philadelphia, PA 19104

First edition published June 2011
Expanded second edition published September 2011

Ebook ISBN: 978-1-61363-006-8
Paperback ISBN: 978-1-61363-005-1

Design by Lara Andrea Taber

Contents

Preface to the Expanded Edition
Leading with the Leader's Checklist

An executive briefs his top management team on plans for the coming year, referencing product launches, pricing pressures, and analyst concerns. The off-site presentation proves engaging and stimulating, yet the moment feels strangely incomplete, an opportunity unfulfilled.

Managers in the room learn little more than they already knew about the executive personally. They hear nothing about how the executive views them collectively or what is expected of them individually. Even worse, they learn much about the tactics of the moment but little about the larger goals and strategies they are pursing. In the end, the executive weaves in many of the essential threads of the leadership fabric but falls short of spinning the whole cloth.

Sound familiar? It should. My work on leadership development in the United States and abroad confirms that meetings like this take place all the time, in a multitude of languages, to the universal consternation of those present. Sometimes the problem is a simple lack of experience: Leading effectively is a composite skillset enhanced by practice. Yet my research and observations suggest that, even when managers are learning on the job, the simple expedient of applying the equivalent of a pilot or surgeon's checklist can mitigate and, in many cases, eliminate leadership lapses, not only in routine matters such as meetings but also when jobs, businesses, and even lives are on the line.

That is why I wrote *The Leader's Checklist*. It lays out a core of 15 mission-critical, time-tested leadership principles that vary surprisingly little among companies or countries. Collectively, these principles are a template for decision-making whatever the challenge, the setting, or the moment.

Continuous Improvement

In Part One, I define the 15 principles that constitute the Leader's Checklist, and together we explore the principles in action, in settings as varied as Wall Street, the Civil War, and an audacious rescue carried out under the glare of international attention. I also provide an Owner's Manual—a set of prompts intended to assist a leader's preparedness for any situation—and I counsel you on how to test and retest your own application of the principles.

The testing is critical. Learning to lead is one of those personal capacities continuously improved by repeated application and accumulated experience. And thus, testing and revising the Leader's Checklist constitutes a learning cycle that helps ensure that all of its principles are essential, complete, and relevant to individual circumstances.

In the relatively brief time since this book was first published, I have heard from scores of managers who have done just that: held these principles up to the reality of their own work lives and the exigencies of the difficult economic times we inhabit. From points far and wide—the United Nations and World Economic Forum, MasterCard and Medtronic, and Eli Lilly and IBM, among others—they have reported back to me about what they feel needs greater emphasis or more tweaking, as well as on what struck home with special force.

This preface to the expanded edition of *The Leader's Checklist* gives me a chance to convey their practical wisdom and direct experience to you, before you dive fully into the checklist itself. Think of this both as a highlighted edition of *The Leader's Checklist,* informed by on-the-ground experience, and as a goad to digest it more critically yourself when you get to the fuller explication of the 15 featured precepts. The principles, I am convinced, are timeless, but like business conditions, the circumstances are ever-changing.

Missing in Action

While *The Leader's Checklist* is defined by 15 principles, multiple managers have let me know that, in their experience, three particular principles have more often been missing in action than others. In some cases, the managers said, they had too seldom or inconsistently utilized them in the exercise of their own leadership. Just as often, they had too infrequently witnessed their use among other leaders who should have embraced them. Either way, the result has been the same: compromised leadership at a moment when an enterprise cannot afford to flounder.

The three principles these managers have found most lacking, in themselves and others:

Honor the Room: Express confidence in and support for those who work for you.

Communicate Persuasively: Communicate in ways that people will never forget.

Place Common Interest First: Common purpose comes first, parochial concerns last.

Why are these three honored more in the breach than in practice? I suspect the answer lies in the fact that so many management cultures do not adequately emphasize or build these three mission-critical principles into their leadership development programs. Whatever the source of the shortfall, however, their absence is keenly felt and sometimes proves disastrous to company reputation, the bottom line, and even the national interest.

Think, for example, of the inability of then–BP chief executive Tony Hayward to communicate persuasively his concern for the environmental impact of his company's ruptured wellhead in the Gulf of Mexico or of the ways in which so many members of the investment banking community appeared to put parochial self-interest ahead of investor and national interest during the financial collapse of 2008.[i]

As for failing to honor the room, look no further than Jeff Kindler, the former CEO of one of the world's largest pharmaceutical companies, Pfizer. By virtually all accounts, Kindler repeatedly confronted, interrogated, criticized, and micro-managed his top managers, even publicly upbraiding a board member. With little real followership in the wake of his consistent failure to honor any room and with negative share performance to show for his efforts, Kindler was bounced by the board less than five years after gaining office.[ii]

Challenging Times

While all 15 principles should be applicable to most moments when leadership is on the line, several take on special salience when facing especially stressful or troubling times: for example, the present. Again drawing on the freshly conveyed experience of managers in a host of settings, the checklist principles most vital for challenging times are:

> **Think and Act Strategically:** Set forth a pragmatic strategy for moving forward both short- and long-term, and ensure that it is widely understood; consider all the players, and anticipate reactions and resistance before they are manifest.

> **Take Charge:** Embrace a bias for action, of taking responsibility even if it is not formally delegated, particularly if you are well positioned to make a difference.

> **Act Decisively:** Make good and timely decisions, and ensure that they are executed.

When so stated, much of this is blindingly obvious, but there is no more important time for leaders to remember to highlight these principles in action than when a company is restructuring, a country is floundering, or a community is struggling. With wild gyrations on the world's stock markets, downgrades and even threatened defaults in sovereign debt, and sputtering recoveries in many national economies, enterprise leaders are all but compelled to redouble their strategic thinking, decisive decision-making, and a willingness to take direct charge.

Imagine, for example, an America is which business leaders took greater charge of reducing the country's persistent 9-plus–percent unemployment rate. With the chance of effective Washington intercession close to nil given the nation's political gridlock, business could make employment a priority. Doing so will require that they build on the tripartite principles of strategic thinking, taking charge, and acting decisively.

Yes, the institutional investors that now control two-thirds of America's publicly traded shares might well take exception—their focus is on delivering near-term shareholder value above all else, while punishing executives and directors who repeatedly fall short.[iii] But what might seem an idée fixe of the American way is really a moment's artifice, a prescription that served a past era but less well the current one.

If Fortune 500 companies, for instance, each added only 1,000 Americans to their payrolls, they could jointly expand U.S. employment by half a million and cut national unemployment by a third of a point. Working together, an inner circle of leading executives, directors, and owners might commit to creating a million new U.S. jobs within the next year or to establishing a research and development fund for innovative ways to expand employment.

Given the billions in cash that many companies have accumulated at home and abroad, the wherewithal for both is already in the bank. When it comes to growth in employment in the United States, a mobilized leadership of those who own and oversee the apex of the private sector could thus help provide it at a time when Washington cannot. To return to the principle in question, this would be taking charge when others seemingly cannot.[iv]

Starting Up

Although the 15 checklist principles have emerged from research and observations of managers in large organizations, the experience of start-up managers also points to the importance of developing a specialized Leader's Checklist for fast-growing enterprises as well.

When Margaret Whitman came in to build eBay in California in 1998, the company employed just 35 people. To her surprise, Whitman found her staff maintained no appointment calendars or virtually any daily structure. None were required for the informal ways in which founder Pierre Omidyar had led the fledgling enterprise. When she departed a decade later, eBay's payroll had soared to 15,000. In terms of foundational principles, the leadership challenges Whitman faced were unchanged; 10 years of growth, though, had altered application of the principles enormously.

An equally abrupt example of radically altered terrain: When Liu Chuanzhi started Lenovo in China in 1984—in a guard house at the Chinese Academy of Sciences—he had just two employees, including himself. Twenty-seven years later, he now runs the world's fourth largest personal-computer company, with more than 22,000 at work. In its earliest days, the company required no formalities of any kind, but as with eBay, successful growth brought a whole new set of applications while simultaneously requiring the consistent application of enduring principles. In Lenovo's case, that meant a weekly review of the decisions of the past five days—a process that has now been underway for nearly three decades. By repeatedly looking back to better see forward, Liu Chuanzhi has built his own Leader's Checklist—

one that helped his company acquire the IBM personal computer division in 2005 and emerge on to the world stage.

Reality Events

Throughout my academic study and my development work in leadership, I have looked at how others perform in their leadership moments—nearby, across the globe, or through the long reach of time. Feedback from managers has shown one avenue of exploration to be of particular interest, especially in a time of often-contradictory media messages: reality events—not the network-television variety, but on-the-scene, first-person accounts of leadership in crisis moments. We often acquire indelible insights about how to lead when we are called to our own leadership moments.

In the pages to come, readers will get a first-hand look into how leaders performed—or failed to perform—during the financial collapse at AIG, the miners' rescue in Chile, and the Civil War surrender at Appomattox. I believe that these accounts show the power of the checklist, and many managers have informed me that they wish I had included more narratives of individuals whose leadership has been both extraordinary and exceptionally instructive. In this expanded version, I have added a second part—Leadership in Action—which includes lengthy interviews that I conducted with two leaders whose experience offer great lessons. For links to the video interviews, visit http://wdp.wharton.upenn.edu/books/the-leaders-checklist.

One interview is with Laurence Golborne, the Chilean Mining Minister who led the dramatic rescue of 33 men trapped for two-plus months more than 2,000 feet below the earth's surface. An earlier interview with Golborne had informed the first edition of *The Leader's Checklist*. The more recent interview, included in this expanded addition, reinforces the first but also fleshes out another of the core checklist principles:

> **Motivate the Troops.** Appreciate the distinctive intentions that people bring, and then build on those diverse motives to draw the best from each.

My original account of Golborne's role in the rescue had placed much emphasis on process—pursuing multiple rescue strategies simultaneously, for instance. In this interview, he also stresses the need to repeatedly remind his rescue team of the "dream," the ultimate purpose of the hard and often tedious work that is the substance of success. "You have to be positive" about the challenge, he said; "You have to be optimistic." And for conveying the determination to succeed, you have "to be with the guys" and "to face them with faith that you are going to be able to solve it."

The new interview also adds weight to a vital point under-stressed in the first edition of *The Leader's Checklist*: The overwhelming importance of sustenance from above. From the first moment of the crisis, Chilean President Sebastián Piñera put himself four-square behind the rescue initiative. "President Piñera committed that we would, with all our effort, find them," Golborne recalled, and "at that moment, I felt empowered to take control."

Forcefully committing the country to the rescue, Golborne said, "was key for the success of this operation." And though the initiative did not seem assured of any success at the outset, the president's unswerving support proved essential for first locating the miners—"one of the best moments in my life," Golborne told me—and then raising them to the surface.[v]

I have included a second interview, also new to this expanded edition. I spoke with Joseph Pfeifer, the Chief of Counterterrorism and Emergency Preparedness for the New York City Fire Department. Pfeifer brings extensive experience in leading others during both ordinary and extraordinary times. As a Citywide Command Chief, he served as incident commander for rescue services in the North Tower of the World Trade Center on 9/11. He has also led development of the fire department's strategic plans and terrorism-preparedness strategy.

My interview with him reinforces the 15 checklist principles but also, as in Golborne's case, offers fresh insights into their application, especially the one that reads:

Act Decisively. Make good and timely decisions, and ensure that they are executed.

Pfeifer was conducting a routine check on a gas leak near the World Trade Center on the morning of September 11, 2001, when—at 8:46 AM—he heard the roar of a low-flying plane as it streaked overhead. Pfeifer looked up in time to see the aircraft smash into the North Tower, and judging by the angle and velocity of approach, he instantly concluded it was not an accident but a terrorist attack.[vi]

"At that moment," Pfeifer reported, "we knew we were going to the biggest fire of our lives," and he immediately radioed for a massive deployment of firefighters and beyond. He then directed the urgent rescue efforts in the main lobby of the North Tower, also known as Tower One, over the following hour, making dozens of rapid-fire decisions to effect rescue of those above. And in keeping with the leader's precept of acting decisively, when the nearby South Tower collapsed at 9:59 AM, Pfeifer instantly radioed up a message to the many firefighters who were then high up bringing people down: "Command to all units in Tower One, evacuate the building!"

The interview also points to two other issues that slipped somewhat beneath the radar in the first edition of *The Leader's Checklist*: The vital importance of having a personal stake in the game, and the critical value of not only taking charge and building a top team but also creating and coordinating a network of teams.

On the first point, Pfeifer describes a firefighter who tracked him down after a three-alarm blaze, simply to say: "Chief, I just want to let you know that I'll follow you down any hallway." As nice as the compliment was, Pfeifer realized that the firefighter was really saying that he was looking to Pfeifer to keep him safe when leading him into harm's way. Equally implicit was the knowledge that the firefighter trusted Pfeifer with his own well-being since he knew that Pfeifer had put his own life on the line in the past. Leadership is not just about giving direction from afar, Pfeifer observes, it is also "about sharing the danger," of having skin in the game, of appreciating personally what others are being asked to do and the risks they face.

On the second point, Pfeifer drew on the terrible events of 9/11 to offer an affirmative message for any leader facing complex, fast-moving, and high-stakes events. Sharing intelligence among diverse parties about rapidly evolving conditions should be a pre-built capacity, well in place before calamity strikes. Equally important for any leader is a readiness to guard against what Pfeifer terms "organizational bias"—in his world, where "firefighters go to firefighters, police go to police," and emergency medical personnel pull inward. What is needed is exactly the opposite. If "command and control" is a foundation for authoritative leadership, Pfeifer concludes from his experience in 9/11 and beyond, complex events require leaders who also "connect, collaborate, and coordinate."

The Leader's Checklist

In Part Two, I have also included an interview that *Knowledge@ Wharton* conducted with me during the week when the book was first published. I speak about why I wrote the book, and I offer additional reflections on the importance of having a Leader's Checklist.

Every author of a book such as this one hopes it will prove useful not only in prosperous times when the living is easy but also in hard times when leadership is often put to a stress test. A message that I recently received suggests that in at least one instance this has been the case.

My correspondent is a manager at a large American concern that decided as a matter of business strategy to exit a business it had excelled at for decades. Here, with some edits, is how the manager described the experience:

> **My charge has been to help manage the exit.** We are now almost a year into the transition with perhaps two-and-a-half years remaining. With this change, over 1,500 employees have been impacted, but not all at once.

The senior leadership team has the constant challenge of directing, engaging, and retaining employees through the time they are needed to do the critical work of continuing to meet customer needs as well as wind down the business. In a blink of an eye last year, employees found their work changing, their leaders changing, and of course, their own personal circumstance changing. They went from a growing, ongoing concern for the business to a "below the line" expense that must be cut. And as a result, just as quickly, leaders have had to adapt how they lead.

I have been through divestitures and wind downs in past roles and know of some of the pitfalls that can come along. And as the program manager, I was fully prepared for the worst that could occur from people and financial results. But with this exit, the results have been remarkable. With very little time to strategize and little information to go on, plans have been met within a few percentage points, financial measures have been met or exceeded, and most important, employee satisfaction and engagement have significantly increased.

It has been amazing to watch the growth in leaders as they have had to employ many of the 15 core principles you have outlined. At the time, they didn't do it because they knew it was part of a list; they did it because it was simply the right thing to do for employees and to manage the business. Still, I found it easy to nod in agreement while reading your book since I had in front of me every day real examples of highly effective leadership in action in a very difficult situation.

I certainly don't wish my correspondent's experience on any reader, but should you find yourself in a parallel situation, where your courage and your company's mettle are being tested by roiling market forces, I hope you will find *The Leader's Checklist* as useful and bolstering. And now on to the 15 principles themselves. ∎

Part One
The Leader's
Checklist

Introduction

Imagine yourself in this position: Less than five months ago, you were summoned from the private sector to join a newly formed national government. Your background is in retail; now you are heading up the nation's mining industry. You are abroad on a state visit, still working to come up to speed, when word reaches you from your home office that there has been a mining disaster—a cave-in deep below, death toll unknown, nearly three dozen missing.

Or envision this situation: For decades, your financial services firm has sailed along. Not only have revenues soared, your company has also earned a treasured AAA credit rating while creating an extraordinary wealth engine: a little giant of a division that insures against debt defaults, including subprime mortgages. Continuing prosperity seems predictable, but suddenly the market implodes. Subprime mortgages turn noxious. Lehman Brothers goes under. Your AAA rating slips to AA, then A-; and with the downgrades, you have to post billions of dollars in collateral that you simply do not have. This boat is sailing straight toward a roaring waterfall, and you are standing at the helm.

Or this one: The enemy has surrendered after a four-year conflict that has left more than half a million dead, and your army commander has assigned you to arrange one of the war's crowning moments, the formal surrender of the enemy's most venerated army. The tone, the texture of the ceremony, the formalities of receiving the enemy— they are entirely for you to craft.

These are not, of course, hypothetical or anonymous events. Laurence Golborne, the new mining minister for the Republic of Chile, was visiting in Ecuador on the night of August 5, 2010, when his chief of staff back in Santiago sent him a simple but urgent text message: "Mine cave-in Copiapó; 33 victims." Twenty-eight hours later, at 3:30 a.m. on August 7, Golborne arrived at the remote site of the mining disaster in the Atacama desert of northern Chile. Soon, hundreds of millions of people around the globe would be witnessing one of the greatest mining rescues of all time.

Like the miners in Chile, American International Group (AIG)—the financial services giant heading for the cataract—was ultimately rescued through direct government intervention. The company was deemed "too big to fail," though it was almost too toxic to save. When the subprime mortgage market in which AIG was deeply invested began to collapse, top AIG executives had taken few protective measures. Their tone-deaf response to the tumultuous events that unfolded left the company vulnerable to one of the greatest corporate collapses in business history.

How different the actions taken by Union officer Joshua Lawrence Chamberlain when Ulysses S. Grant handed him the historic duty of coordinating a follow-up ceremony to Robert E. Lee's April 9, 1865, surrender at

Appomattox. Instead of humiliating the Confederate army, as might have been expected after four years of civil war, Chamberlain ordered a respectful salute and launched a healing process that would help reunite a country.

Two of the leaders we have just met were well prepared when summoned to moments of crisis. The other, recent history shows us, was obviously not. To be sure, few of us are likely to have our mettle tested in such trying circumstances. But all of us can and should prepare for less-public crises in our own spheres of serving, and thus it behooves us to ask why: Why did Laurence Golborne and Joshua Chamberlain rise so effectively to the challenge? Why were the AIG executives unable to steer an effective course? Is the skill set that served Golborne and Chamberlain teachable, even transferable and applicable, to leaders who will never be called to scale the kinds of mountains these men had to face?

The animating premise of this book is that effective leadership can be learned, and indeed should be learned, by those with responsibility for the performance of their enterprises and their employees. The further premise is that leadership benefits from an approach built upon specific guiding principles that, taken together, create a clear road map for navigating any situation. That is why I advocate and in these pages lay out the Leader's Checklist, a complete set of vital leadership principles that are tried, tested, and true.

The Leader's Checklist is composed of 15 core principles applicable to most leaders, in most endeavors, in most circumstances. I provide guidance to help you customize this list to specific situations and missions. Given the vast diversity of leadership roles, one size definitely does not fit all in this endeavor. Taken collectively, the Leader's Checklist and its precepts should prepare you well for building an enterprise in good times but also for facing a worst-case leadership scenario, even if (thankfully) you are never called to face one. Finally, I offer an Owner's Manual, so you can put these principles to practice in your own domain of leadership. ■

The Leader's Checklist

A checklist is only as good as its underlying foundation, and the foundation is only as solid as the materials and engineering that go into it. To build the Leader's Checklist, I have tapped not only my own experience but also that of an array of investigators, researchers, thinkers, and practitioners.

From development work with hundreds of managers and executives in leadership programs in Asia, Europe, North America, and South America, from research interviews with many managers in the United States and abroad, and from witnessing managers facing a range of critical moments, I have concluded that their thinking and experience point to a core of just 15 mission-critical leadership principles that vary surprisingly little between companies or countries.[1]

From my own reading, too, I have become convinced that with leadership, as with much else, brevity is the soul of wit. Albert Einstein once described the calling of modern physics as an effort to make the physical universe as simple as possible—but not simpler. The Leader's Checklist is likewise at its best when it is as bare-bones as possible—but not more so. I have tried to hold to that in these pages.[2]

Working with participants in a wide range of leadership programs has also been critical. I asked them how they would lead. I put them in a manager's shoes at a particularly challenging leadership moment. I elicit their experience-based, pragmatic knowledge of what they view as requisite for the effective exercise of leadership.

One such moment that works consistently well to draw out the core principles centers on the then-chief executive of IBM, Louis Gerstner, at a time when he had just acquired software maker Lotus Development Corporation for $3.5 billion. The acquisition had been resisted by Lotus at first, but its chief executive and board accepted the takeover after IBM sweetened its initial offer a week later by more than 10 percent.

The day after the purchase was announced, Gerstner traveled from IBM's headquarters in Armonk, New York, to Boston to meet with half the Lotus workforce, which had been assembled by the outgoing Lotus CEO to help employees learn what their future held. Many were skeptical about their takeover by a computer hardware company with little experience in software development, and many were worried about relocations and layoffs. Even before the acquisition, Lotus had announced a plan to cut 15 percent of its managerial ranks, and IBM itself had been undergoing a massive restructuring and downsizing in the wake of its own struggles at the time. For Lotus employees, now the property of IBM, there was plenty to be anxious and doubtful about.

I ask one of the program participants to take the role of Lou Gerstner at the assemblage, and the other program participants to listen as if they were the anxious and skeptical

Lotus employees. After witnessing the reenactment, which includes a round of questions for the CEO from employees, I then ask participants what they as Lotus workers would want to learn from and about the IBM chief executive, their new leader, if they were to remain with the merged companies and work harder during the coming months.[3]

An even dozen leadership principles emerge from this exercise, and they do so consistently—whether the managers are working in investment banking, high technology, or public service; whether they are functioning in good times or bad; and whether they are located in China, India, or the United States. I have become convinced that these principles should find a place on any Leader's Checklist regardless of period or locale. Indeed, these principles constitute, in my view, the vital foundation of a universally applicable Leader's Checklist. Three additional principles emerge from the accounts with which I began this volume.

15 Mission-Critical Principles

1. **Articulate a Vision.** Formulate a clear and persuasive vision and communicate it to all members of the enterprise.

2. **Think and Act Strategically.** Set forth a pragmatic strategy for achieving that vision both short- and long-term, and ensure that it is widely understood; consider all the players, and anticipate reactions and resistance before they are manifest.

3. Honor the Room. Frequently express your confidence in and support for those who work with and for you.

4. Take Charge. Embrace a bias for action, of taking responsibility even if it is not formally delegated, particularly if you are well positioned to make a difference.

5. Act Decisively. Make good and timely decisions, and ensure that they are executed.

6. Communicate Persuasively. Communicate in ways that people will not forget; simplicity and clarity of expression help.

7. Motivate the Troops. Appreciate the distinctive intentions that people bring, and then build on those diverse motives to draw the best from each.

8. Embrace the Front Lines. Delegate authority except for strategic decisions, and stay close to those most directly engaged with the work of the enterprise.

9. Build Leadership in Others. Develop leadership throughout the organization.

10. Manage Relations. Build enduring personal ties with those who look to you, and work to harness the feelings and passions of the workplace.

11. Identify Personal Implications. Help everybody appreciate the impact that the vision and strategy are likely to have on their own work and future with the firm.

12. Convey Your Character. Through gesture, commentary, and accounts, ensure that others appreciate that you are a person of integrity.

13. Dampen Over-Optimism. Counter the hubris of success, focus attention on latent threats and unresolved problems, and protect against the tendency for managers to engage in unwarranted risk.

14. Build a Diverse Top Team. Leaders need to take final responsibility, but leadership is also a team sport best played with an able roster of those collectively capable of resolving all the key challenges.

15. Place Common Interest First. In setting strategy, communicating vision, and reaching decisions, common purpose comes first, personal self-interest last.

Multiple sources affirm the importance of these core principles, including studies of the qualities of leadership by academic investigators, reviews of leadership development programs among well-established organizations, and consideration of what leaders report has served them well. Here is a brief sampling of sources that corroborate the 15 principles:

Principles 1 (Articulate a Vision), 2 (Think and Act Strategically), and 3 (Honor the Room). Two well-informed observers, educator Howard Gardner and researcher Emma Laskin, explored historical sources on twentieth-century luminaries ranging from Nelson Mandela and

Mahatma Gandhi to Margaret Thatcher and George C. Marshall, and concluded that their common leadership threads included an exceptional ability to define a compelling vision for change, devise a strategy for achieving it, and honor those followers who were being asked to achieve it.[4]

Principles 4 (Take Charge) and 5 (Act Decisively). The U.S. Marine Corps Officer Candidates School places great emphasis on taking charge and acting decisively. To build an ability to make rapid decisions under stress with incomplete information, would-be Marine commanders learn to make do with a "70-percent" solution, not 100-percent consensus; explain unambiguous objectives and leave their subordinates to work out the details; tolerate mistakes if they point to stronger performance next time and are not repeated a second time; and view indecisiveness as a fatal flaw—worse than making a mediocre decision, because a middling decision, swiftly executed, can at least be corrected. In a similar vein, Warren Bennis, an academic observer and a university administrator, concluded that effective leaders were most often defined by a driving determination to reach a goal, an ability to generate trust and communicate optimism, and a bias for action when ambiguity prevails.[5]

Principle 6 (Communicate Persuasively). Drawing on what leaders themselves report is also a rich lode. There is no shortage of leaders willing to reveal what has worked, or sometimes failed, in their own exercise of power. Inevitably, some of these accounts are exercises in vanity, self-promotion, or self-justification, but the best of such self-reporting furnishes useful insights from the front lines of leadership. CEO Dawn Lepore of online retailer Drugstore.com, with revenue in 2010 of $450 million, offered that while she was "very comfortable with ambiguity," when "you're leading a large organization, people are not as comfortable with ambiguity, and they want you to be clearer about what's happening, where you're taking them. So I had to get better at communicating what I was thinking." Communicating must also be two-way, reported Carol Bartz, CEO of Internet provider Yahoo, who saw the act of hearing as essential, if not always natural: "I have a bad habit—you get half your question out and I think I know the whole question, so I want to answer it. And so I actually had to be trained to take a breath. I really want to listen. I want to engage, but I have to shut up."[6]

Principles 7 (Motivate the Troops), 8 (Embrace the Front Lines), and 9 (Build Leadership in Others). Peter Drucker, who studied managers in action over six decades, deemed effective leaders to be those who delegated much but retained authority over what was most strategic for the organization. But effective leaders also had a habit of personally visiting the front lines, giving rise to the title of one of Drucker's publications on the subject, "Not Enough Generals Were Killed," a slighting reference to World War I army commanders who remained far from the battle lines while ordering soldiers into pointless rounds of trench warfare. To Noel Tichy, a university professor who also directed General Electric's leadership program for several years, building troop strength is a matter of creating other leaders throughout the organization. American Express, China Mobile, General Electric, and many other organizations have created and refined such programs to instill leadership across the ranks.[7]

Principles 10 (Manage Relations), 11 (Identify Personal Implications), and 12 (Convey Your Character). Frances Hesselbein, who led the Girl Scouts for more than a decade and then led an organization for nonprofit leadership, emphasized the value of personal mentoring, flattening the hierarchy, and hearing dissent. For researcher Daniel Goleman, vital qualities are exceptional self-awareness, self-regulation, and personal empathy, a combination that he has termed emotional intelligence. An academic team that studied middle managers in financial services, food processing, and telecommunications in 62 countries, ranging from Albania to Zimbabwe, concluded that leaders should avoid developing autocratic, egocentric, and irritable styles.[8]

Principles 13, 14, and 15. I share accounts later in the book that underscore the value of the three final principles. ■

Customizing the Leader's Checklist

The 15 principles provide a solid foundation for a Leader's Checklist, suitable for most leadership moments at most organizations at most times. But "most" is not always good enough. Customized checklists are required for distinct times and contexts. Among the most important divisions are those of company, role, country, moment, and personal place.

Company. Every organization requires its own customized set of checklist principles. In recent years, many of the largest have established such lists.

The Leader's Checklist for General Electric, according to those highly familiar with the company, would include, for instance, teaching others how to lead their divisions, making tough—often wrenching—personnel decisions around performance, and continually innovating. A checklist for Google, by contrast, would place greater emphasis on pursuing individual creative sparks, keeping teams small, and guiding others in an even-keeled manner. A checklist for a major professional services firm might identify nearly a dozen special capacities that it holds to be vital for its managers, including seeing the world through clients' eyes, enthusiastically engaging with clients, and working with them to transcend conventional thinking.

Role. Distinct positions necessitate their own unique additions to the core Leader's Checklist. The customized principles for top executives are different from those for frontline managers. They, in turn, are different from those for company directors.

In interviewing more than a hundred company executives and institutional investors—part of a study of how the two work together or are sometimes at odds with each other—I found a special demand for chief executives to build personal familiarity with their largest investors, articulate a compelling vision for where the company was going and a persuasive strategy for getting there, and generate steady quarterly and annual growth in company earnings. In a separate study of company directors, a professional colleague and I learned that many directors place a premium on partnering with—not just monitoring—management, establishing clear lines between decisions retained by the board and those delegated to management, and taking an active role in setting company strategy.

In sum, a customized Leader's Checklist for CEOs would include building relations with investors, making a persuasive case for how the company will create additional shareholder value, and then delivering steady and predictable growth in quarterly and annual earnings. The customized Leader's Checklist for company directors, by contrast, might include an ability to both partner with and monitor company executives, guide company strategy, and create a bright line between delegated decisions and retained authority.[9]

Country. Specific principles are essential for varied national locations as well. What is required in China or India is at least partially distinct from what is essential in America or Brazil.

This can be seen in the findings of the study of leadership styles in 67 countries cited earlier. Working to engage rather than just instruct others drew high marks in countries such as the United States. By contrast, a greater premium is placed on indirect forms of communication through metaphors, parables, and the like in China.[10]

In pursuit of such customized principles for leading business in India, in 2007-09 three colleagues and I interviewed senior executives at 100 of the largest 150 Indian publicly traded companies. Among our interviewees was R. Gopalakrishnan, executive director of Tata Sons, which oversees Tata Group, India's largest company in market capitalization, with interests in automobiles, communication, consulting, hotels, power, steel, and tea. Drawing upon his experience in presiding over 300,000 employees and revenue equal to 3 percent of India's GDP, Gopalakrishnan told us that Indian executives like himself had adopted many Western leadership principles but also embraced distinctly Indian qualities in running their enterprises.

For the Indian manager, Gopalakrishnan observed, "his intellectual tradition, his y axis, is Anglo-American," but "his action vector, his x axis, is in the Indian ethos." Many "foreigners come to India," he said, "they talk to Indian managers, and they find them very articulate, very analytical, very smart, very intelligent. And then they can't for the life of them figure out why the Indian manager can't do something about [the plan] as prescribed by the analysis."

Indian business leaders, he concluded, "think in English" but "act Indian."

The core leadership principles of the kinds summarized earlier are much the same in both the United States and India, we have found, and I believe that they are essential for running business firms in all major economies. Company leaders everywhere emphasize company strategy and motivating the work force, both on the y axis. Yet our study of Indian executives also revealed that they generally embraced four distinctive principles, all on an x axis, constituting a kind of "India Way" for leading business on that subcontinent:[11]

- *Holistic engagement with employees.* Indian business leaders see their firms as organic enterprises where sustaining employee morale and building company culture are critical obligations. People are viewed as assets to be developed, not costs to be reduced.

- *Improvisation and adaptability.* Improvisation is also at the heart of the India Way. In a complex, often volatile environment with few resources and much red tape, business leaders have learned to rely on their wits to circumvent recurrent and innumerable hurdles.

- *Creative value propositions.* Given the large and intensely competitive domestic market, Indian business leaders have of necessity learned to create value propositions that satisfy the needs of demanding consumers and do so with extreme efficiency.

• *Broad mission and purpose.* Indian business leaders place special emphasis on personal values, a vision of growth, and strategic thinking. They take pride in not only enterprise success but also family prosperity, regional advance, and national renaissance.

Moment. The same need for customization of the Leader's Checklist applies to moment as well. What is essential in changing times is at least partially different from what is required in static times. What is needed in hard times is different from the requisite list for good times. Distinctive principles can also be essential for leading during varied phases of an organization's experience, ranging from periods of start-up and rapid growth to sudden contraction or unwanted acquisition.

For leading organizational change, for example, academic John Kotter and consultant Dan Cohen have offered up an eight-step template—checklist principles that those leading the change would be wise to embrace. These include the creation of a compelling rationale for change and small steps that pave the way for greater transformation. Each step requires graphic portrayal, such as hearing directly from distressed customers in building a "burning platform" for change.[12]

For leading companies during a sharp downdraft, by contrast, consider the customized checklist that emerged from a study of large American firms during the financial crisis of 2008–09. Along with two colleagues, I interviewed 14 chief executives of major, publicly traded American companies during the height of the financial crisis in 2009. We asked the CEOs what they deemed critical to the leadership of their firms during a period of nearly unprecedented cutbacks, furloughs, and layoffs brought on by the failures of Lehman Brothers, AIG, Merrill Lynch, and other financial services firms.

Interviewees included the chief executives of DuPont, Northrop Grumman, Procter & Gamble, 3M, Travelers, and Tyco. While each emphasized steps unique to his or her own firm, most also stressed eight add-on principles. One, for instance, was to devote extra time and attention to the firm's clientele. As A. G. Lafley, then-chief executive of Procter & Gamble, put it: "A lesson I would give others on how to manage through tough times is to stay close to your customers." Another was to swiftly recognize the hard reality and get on with corrective actions, as Tyco CEO Ed Breen described it: "You have to get as much data as quickly as possible. But you will never get it all—so you need to make decisions quickly." The distinctive leadership principles for stressful times, as articulated by this set of chief executives, included reaffirming the mission but confronting reality, sustaining faith in recovery and the future, and concentrating on what you can control.[13]

Still other customized checklists are required for leading other kinds of institutions, ranging from universities and nonprofit organizations to religious movements, school systems, sports teams, community services, micro-finance institutions, and agencies such as the United Nations.[14] Mission-specific checklists are also essential for leading laterally with peers and partners, and upwardly with top managers and directors.[15]

Personal Place. While core and customized principles constitute a kind of "true north" for every manager, each Leader's Checklist must also be customized for one's personal place. No two leadership positions are exactly the same, nor do any two sets of circumstances require the identical exercise of leadership. By way of illustration, here are three checklists that have been customized for personal place.

- *Patrolling.* A commanding officer created a set of checklists in 2009–10 for his infantry units operating in Afghanistan. Termed "tactical standard operating procedures," they referenced actions required of officers operating in the field at a variety of points, ranging from reconnaissance and bivouacking to escalating force and medical evacuation. The Patrol Leader checklist, for example, required that soldiers obtain a clear statement of mission from their commanding officer before embarking on the patrol, identify not only a primary route but also a backup itinerary in case of hostile fire, and coordinate in advance with those who might be called upon to provide air or artillery support. U.S. Army officers have created a website to compile and share a host of such leadership guidelines from those who are serving on the front lines.[16]

- *Firefighting.* U.S. wildland firefighting services have generated a set of checklists for teams working to suppress forest, grass, and other fires in the wilderness. One checklist requires that incident commanders have affirmative responses to three questions before launching a fire attack: Are controls in place for identifiable hazards? Are the planned tactics suitable given the anticipated fire behavior? Have unambiguous instructions been given to and understood by the firefighters? Similarly, the Fire Department of New York City provides 13 checklists for officers responsible for major incidents, including a Mayday Checklist that requires ordering all unrelated two-way radio traffic to cease, establishing a staging area, and enlisting chaplains as needed.[17]

• *Selling.* Two Microsoft sales managers adapted a pilot's pre-flight checklist to a pre-sales checklist, asking before a sales call that their representatives Google all who are expected at the meeting, submit their two-minute opening pitch to memory, and listen during the meeting to learn about the personalities in the room and the politics of the firm.[18] ∎

Testing the Leader's Checklist

Taken together, the core and customized Leader's Checklists should serve as a useful starting foundation for managers. But in a dynamic world, the principles will always remain subject to change and improvement through recurrent testing and frequent refinement. Careful evaluation of the leadership principles can even at times call for a surprising rewiring.

Human resource managers at Google, for example, had anticipated that possessing technology expertise would be an important principle for leading at the company. Yet on testing what proved most effective with employees, Google researchers found that seven other leadership abilities had greater impact, including a capacity to articulate a strategy and to foster others' career development.[19]

In a study of the leadership at a major division of a large financial services firm, two fellow researchers and I uncovered the need for a similar revision in the customized checklist principles deemed to be most vital at that firm. One of our colleagues interviewed virtually all the top executives of a 4,000-person division, and from those interviews he identified 200 distinct capacities that at least some bankers viewed as valuable for leading the operation. When he then asked the division leaders to rank the 200, the banking executives consistently placed 39 at the top.

Our colleague then took two additional testing steps that resulted in a surprising reconfiguration of the Leader's Checklist for this division. He first asked the leaders' peers, direct reports, and superiors to rate each of the leaders on all 39 capacities. Next, he looked at the financial results of the leaders a year later, knowing that their performance depended upon whether they could muster and align the energy of the bankers who reported to them.

With this data in hand, we found that only nine of the 39 identified leadership capacities had a significant impact on financial performance of the banking leaders. Qualities that were once highly rated, such as demonstrating strong commitment to company success, establishing a team-based sales culture, and streamlining the sales process, fell away when the baseline financial test was applied. Not surprisingly, the bank division subsequently focused its leadership development programs on a customized Leader's Checklist that comprised the nine principles that did make a difference—including the personal mentoring and motivating of the frontline bankers—and not the other 30 principles, a radical reconfiguring from what the bank had initially expected.[20]

Systematic study does not always confirm the status quo or even what is intuitively accepted. Sometimes, a hard look serves to upend or alter conventional, perhaps outdated wisdom. Testing the Leader's Checklist can thus be invaluable not only for confirming its principles but also for evolving and revising them. ■

Activating the Leader's Checklist

Would you have surgery performed by a doctor who routinely failed to confirm that the right patient was in the operating room and the correct procedure was about to be performed? Or willingly fly with a pilot who regularly failed to check wind speed, flight plan, and all the other essential ingredients for ensuring a successful takeoff?

Obviously not. Medical centers often require physicians to run through a specific checklist before commencing surgery. Aviation authorities around the globe require the same of pilots before takeoff. Indeed, in many newer jetliners, a commercial pilot is not given full access to the controls until the checklist process has been electronically confirmed. To be sure, mistakes still get made on the runway and in the operating room, sometimes horrible ones, but since every item on each of these lists is critical, mandating them all is a sensible guarantee against missing any, as Atul Gawande's *The Checklist Manifesto* and recent research have made clear.[21]

How surprising, then, that those in leadership positions often fail to require the equivalent of themselves. We take for granted a pilot's thoroughness, or a surgeon's, but we too often give ourselves a pass on reviewing an analogous list, or merely having one to check, even when we are facing moments during which a complete leadership inventory might be essential for sensibly directing or even saving the enterprise.

If executive compensation could somehow be directly linked both to creating a personalized Leader's Checklist *and* routinely applying it—in the same way pilots have to move through a checklist before being allowed to proceed to the next phase of flight—I am certain there would be far fewer botched takeoffs and landings, and fewer midflight failures, in the corporate arena. But with no comparable authority or device insisting on the Leader's Checklist, the enterprising manager must enforce one's own compliance.

For application to occur, however, managers must work to overcome a host of predictable but preventable behavioral lapses. One of the most important is that of knowing what should be done but then failing to do it, what researchers Jeffrey Pfeffer and Robert Sutton have termed the "knowing-doing gap." Even the best checklist has no value unless it is routinely activated to guide a leader's behavior. Doing so for many managers is an acquired rather than a natural skill.[22]

Drawing on both academic research and interviews with organizational leaders, I have found that managers fruitfully engage in six learning avenues that help them activate the Leader's Checklist on a regular basis:

1) Study leadership moments.
2) Solicit coaching and mentoring.
3) Accept stretch experiences.
4) Conduct after-action reviews of personal leadership moments.

5) Endure extremely stressful leadership moments.
6) Experience the leadership moments of others.

1. Study leadership moments.

A first step for learning to apply the Leader's Checklist is to become a self-directed student of leadership. This study can take many forms: reading leaders' biographies, witnessing leaders in action, and joining leadership development programs. What's critical is witnessing how others have worked with a full checklist or fallen short, often a powerful reminder to examine whether you yourself are employing all the necessary principles. In my leadership development programs, for instance, I often draw upon the experience of teams of firefighters whose commanders invited disaster by employing a less-than-full checklist.

I also frequently employ the following illustration from the pharmaceutical industry, one of the most informative moments I have ever studied for what it reveals about the value of a Leader's Checklist.[23]

The director of research and development (R&D) at Merck, the giant U.S.-based pharmaceutical company, faced a critical decision. A scientist proposed developing a drug to combat a terrible disease called River Blindness. Hundreds of thousands had already lost their eyesight, and 20 million were at risk. Since the new treatment would be based on modification of an existing Merck product, a decision to invest might seem obvious—were it not for the fact that most of the victims lived in rural Nigeria and other poverty-stricken areas of west Africa. They could simply not afford the drug if it were developed, whatever its sight-saving powers. Even worse for Merck as a commercial enterprise was the fact that if it created a cure, it was likely to find itself pressured to pay for its manufacturing and distribution to millions of victims living in some of the remotest regions of Africa.[24]

This might seem like a nonstarter for anybody with responsibility for the near-term performance of a publicly traded company. But quarterly and annual returns were only one of the R&D director's priorities. He also required long-term strategic thinking on behalf of the company, and that focused his attention on building income streams for years in the future. This line of thinking led him to conclude as well that although Merck would in fact have to give the drug away once it was developed, the company would ultimately gain. Given a strengthened reputation among doctors and regulators, renewed ability to recruit top scientists, and fresh brand recognition in countries like Nigeria, where Merck would long be remembered for its generosity, the company was likely to more than make up for its immediate losses in producing a drug that no customers could afford.

With a balanced focus on both short-term returns and long-term gains as part of his checklist principle of strategic thinking, the director of R&D decided to invest in the sight-saving product. And while it was indeed costly in the near term, it proved providential over the decades. When the company sought scientists for its R&D operation years later, the fact that it had combated River Blindness at its own expense proved a powerful recruitment tool. Merck's seeming "loss-leader" decision also helped make it a consistent winner in *Fortune* magazine's annual listing of America's most admired companies. And in the future, a significant portion of Nigeria's 140 million people might well give preference to Merck's products over those of rivals because of the cure's free distribution to some 10 million of their compatriots exposed to River Blindness. Although Merck did not explicitly follow a Leader's Checklist at the time, the company's success demonstrates the effectiveness of an ordered, principles-based approach.

2. Solicit coaching and mentoring.

Solicit personal feedback from individuals who can provide informed, fine-grained advice on not only the leadership capacities that you already exhibit but those that require better display. It is hard to correct what you do not know you are not doing.

3. Accept stretch experiences.

Ask for and accept new responsibilities outside your comfort zone. By testing fresh territories and experiencing the setbacks they can bring, you can grow to appreciate the shortfalls in your own Leader's Checklist even as you learn to more consistently apply it. The absence of strategic thinking and honoring the room, for example, are not so evident in the early years of a career, but the diverse experiences that come with expanding responsibilities often strengthen the need to apply such principles, especially after one personally witnesses the costs of not doing so.

4. Conduct after-action reviews of personal leadership moments.

Look back on leadership actions just taken, asking what worked, what was not invoked, and even what was missing from the Leader's Checklist. Such after-action reviews have been critical to the success of the Chinese computer maker Lenovo. At the end of every week since the company's founding in 1984, chief executive Liu Chuanzhi and his top aides have reviewed their decisions of the past five days, looking to identify what they did well and did not do well in order to avoid repeating what has been done poorly. Through such consistent application, Liu has built a Leader's Checklist that helped his company acquire the IBM personal computer division in 2005 and emerge as the world's fourth largest computer maker in the years since.[25]

5. Endure extremely stressful leadership moments.

Transform a chilling experience into a learning opportunity. We often learn as much from setbacks as successes—sometimes we learn even more from setbacks than successes— and with unflinching study of the stumbles, you should have a greater readiness to apply the Leader's Checklist the next time you are required to do so. This is partly why Cisco Systems' John Chambers had been one of the longest surviving chief executives in Silicon Valley. Chambers took the Cisco helm in 1995 and rode the Internet wave in the late 1990s to make his company one of the world's most valued entities, with a market capitalization soaring above $500 billion. But when the Internet bubble burst at the end of that decade, Cisco flipped from extraordinary growth to stunning contraction. Chambers and Cisco survived the collapse, and he attributed much of the company's success in the decade that followed to what he learned when it felt as if he were touching the void.[26]

6. Experience the leadership moments of others.

The final step is to vicariously or directly experience a leadership moment when application of the Leader's Checklist is much in order. When you walk in another's shoes during a critical test of leadership or replicate such a moment in microcosm, you will build a better appreciation for when and how to invoke the Leader's Checklist—and underscore what may still be missing from the checklist. To appreciate how a study of leadership moments can influence the development of the Leader's Checklist, read on.

Leadership Failure: Mismanaging Risk at AIG

What happens when there is no Leader's Checklist, or no attempt to fully apply one? Sometimes, very little. As every manager learns with cathartic relief, there are times when muddling through works just fine. But the higher the stakes, the more dire the consequences if a leader goes into a moment unprepared and the muddling falls short. For graphic illustration, American International Group's financial meltdown of 2008 is hard to top.

   Under the leadership of just three chief executives since its founding in 1919, AIG had by 2007 become one of the world's most successful companies. With more than 100,000 employees and annual revenue exceeding $100 billion, the company ranked 10th on the Fortune 500 list, ahead of

Goldman Sachs and not far behind Citigroup. AIG had become one of the 30 blue-chip companies that defined the Dow Jones Industrial Average.

A key driver of AIG's ascent had been one of its newer and smaller divisions, Financial Products (AIGFP). AIG's chief executive created the division in 1987 in response to rising demand for protection against debt defaults. Other financial institutions had been rapidly expanding their debt holdings, and AIGFP stepped forward to write insurance against their failure. Customers were promised that AIG would make them whole on defaults in securities ranging from auto loans and credit card receivables to subprime mortgages and credit default obligations.

At the outset, AIGFP charged relatively modest fees— in some cases just 0.02 cent per year for each dollar of insured risk—but across billions of dollars in such policies, it proved to be a lucrative business. Slow at first to grow, Financial Products accounted for only 4 percent of AIG's operating income by 1999, a dozen years after its launch. Over the next six years, though, AIGPF's share soared to 17 percent of the parent company's operating income. With fewer than 400 employees, AIGFP eventually came to back more than $1.5 trillion in credit default obligations, including some $58 billion in mortgage-backed securities—in all, the equivalent of well over half the GDP of France.[27]

The rapid growth in AIGFP earnings appeared to come with just modest risk to the company. AIG's chief executive reported to a group of investors in 2007 that the firm's risk metrics were "very reliable" and that they provided management with "a very high level of comfort." The head of AIGFP affirmed that promise: "We believe this is a money-good portfolio" and "the models we use are simple, they're specific and they're highly conservative." Enterprise risks, he added, were acceptable: "It is hard for us, without being flippant, to even see a scenario within any kind of realm of reason that would see us losing one dollar in any of those transactions."[28]

As they built the business, AIGFP executives learned that they could back large portfolios of debt at competitive rates in part because their parent held an AAA credit rating, the highest grade. Bestowed on just a handful of firms, it proved an invaluable advantage. Under the prevailing practice at the time, AIGFP was not obligated to set aside cash or assets to back its obligations because of its AAA status. If any of the insured debt defaulted, the company would of course have to pay its customers, but, using historical data, executives calculated that they could readily muster the cash that would be required to cover the relatively small number of losses expected at any given time. And the AAA rating assured customers that AIG could indeed meet those obligations.

That calculus, however, proved lethal. After investment bank Lehman Brothers failed, on September 15, 2008, institutional investors and rating agencies turned to see if other companies held large amounts of the toxic subprime mortgages that had pushed Lehman over the edge. AIGFP did, and on September 15, a major rating agency dropped AIG to A-. Because of the industry convention of requiring collateral if an insurer was rated only A, the downgrade instigated massive collateral calls from AIGFP's customers, some $18 billion in just hours after Lehman's collapse from banking heavyweights such as Barclays, Deutsche Bank, and Goldman Sachs.[29]

Investors rushed to sell their AIG shares, sending the company's stock plummeting by 60 percent in one day. The resulting credit concerns brought on a requirement that AIGFP post still another $15 billion. To cover the mushrooming demands for collateral, AIG was forced to draw $28 billion on September 17 from an emergency U.S. fund created the night before. Still further losses followed, $32 billion by the end of September and another $61 billion by end of the year, the largest annual shortfall in corporate history. The U.S. ultimately injected more than $170 billion to save the firm and assumed control of nearly 80 percent of its voting shares.

How to explain such a spectacular collapse? Historically bad market forces were certainly in play in 2008, as were unusually good times before that. With the long-serving Maurice Greenberg at the helm until 2005, the firm had repeatedly found advantage in entering risky markets worldwide where others did not, from insuring Russian trade to Nigerian oil. Strategic resourcefulness and audacious expansion had helped lift the company up to the Dow 30 and Fortune 10. But it is the duty of top management to anticipate bad times as well as good ones, and that is precisely where a thorough Leader's Checklist could have prevented or drastically softened AIG's fall.

Greenberg and his successor, for example, had extended the London-based Financial Products division a leash that proved far too lengthy, especially in light of how the division's aggressive instincts had already been blessed by AIG's executives and board. AIGFP employees reported that their division president had received relatively little oversight from the company CEO and that the chief executive in turn received scant oversight from the directors. The board's limited vigilance in turn may have stemmed from AIG's relatively weak governance at the time. Not long before the fall, a governance-rating agency had given AIG governance a nearly failing grade of D.[30]

Company leaders had been repeatedly warned of the exceptional risks that its Financial Products division was taking. One federal regulator, for example, reported in 2005 to the AIG governing board that it had found "weaknesses in AIGFP's documentation of complex structures transactions, in policies and procedures regarding accounting, in stress testing, in communication of risk tolerances, and in the company's outline of lines of authority, credit risk management and measurement." Regulators came back in 2007, now warning of mounting subprime mortgage dangers and insisting that the board improve AIGFP's internal controls. AIG's outside auditor in 2008 found fault with a host of its accounting practices.[31]

In hindsight, it is easy to understand why the company CEO and division president paid so little attention to admonitions from the regulators, auditors, and increasingly the market itself. AIGFP was a shooting star whose rapid expansion contributed mightily to its parent company's results and assured annual bonuses across the board. We know from academic studies that company success can result in excessive confidence and risk taking, and we know from human nature that we are loath to look a gift horse in the mouth. What's more, robust growth traditionally has led to unrealistic appraisals of latent risks, particularly low-probability, high-impact threats that can prove catastrophic.[32]

Yet since this is, in fact, a clearly marked and predictable path of human behavior, one of the obligations of AIG's leadership was to recognize such behavioral shortcomings *before* they could wreak havoc on the enterprise. If the AIGFP president was not heeding the warning signs of excessive risk, that responsibility fell to his boss, the AIG chief executive. And if the chief executive was unable to foresee the gathering storm, the board was duty-bound to guard against his over-optimism. Intervention at any one of these levels might have helped prevent a catastrophe of historic proportions, while the absence of such intervention at every level virtually assured it.

The 13th principle of the Leader's Checklist is readily drawn from this account. It will help leaders see beyond and around the momentary euphoria of flush times so they can concentrate on steering an enterprise through both the prosperous and the hard years ahead.

---

13. Dampen Over-Optimism. Counter the hubris of success, focus attention on latent threats and unresolved problems, and protect against the tendency for managers to engage in unwarranted risks.

Leadership Triumph: Rescuing Miners in Chile

If AIG's collapse is a story of unmitigated disaster, the 2010 rescue of 33 trapped Chilean miners is its polar opposite, a tale of unalloyed success. Regardless of outcome, I believe that close study of leadership at its worst and at its best is an essential source of fresh insights into what is essential for a complete Leader's Checklist, and the miners' rescue in Chile is certainly among the finest examples available in recent years. It reinforces the value of the consistent use of the Leader's Checklist for guiding action—and underscores still another principle for the core checklist.[33]

Laurence Golborne made his mark as chief executive of Chile's largest retail chain, Cencosud, an enterprise with more than 10,000 employees and annual turnover of $10 billion. In early 2010, the newly elected president of Chile, Sebastián Piñera, asked Golborne to serve with him as the nation's mining minister, and they took office together on March 11, 2010.[34]

Though he had initially questioned whether he should accept the government ministry in the absence of any prior experience in the industry, Golborne believed that his management know-how would more than make up for the lack of technical grounding. The mining ministry is "where I can contribute my management skills," he had explained to his family. And now, without miner rescue experience either, he would eventually conclude that his management capacities were enough for him to assume responsibility for rescuing the 33 miners trapped in the Atacama. "Although I do not come from the mining world," Golborne explained, "and was questioning myself what I could do in the mine—how I could help in the rescue given the magnitude of the problem—I understood I had to be there." But getting to that point entailed a wrenching encounter.[35]

Golborne arrived at the San José mine, the scene of the disaster, two days after the cave-in, uncertain about the role he should play but determined to see the situation for himself. Later that same day, a rescue team returned from the depths and reported that the entire mine had become so unstable that nobody could safely enter most of it for any reason, let alone descending all the way down to the stranded miners some 2,000 feet below. A member of the rescue squad confided to the mining minister, "They must be dead," and "if they are not dead, they will die."

In the interest of transparency, Golborne decided to immediately disclose the bleak appraisal to the miners' relatives who had converged at the mine's entry. But when he noticed two daughters of one of the trapped miners weeping after he reported the dispiriting assessment, he lost his own composure and for a moment could not continue. "Minister, you cannot break down," shouted one of the relatives. "You have to give us strength!" For Golborne, it became a turning point. The meeting with the miners' families ended his ambivalence about whether he and the government of Chile should assume direct authority over the rescue, even though the accident had occurred at a privately owned mine—and despite the fact that the nation's top mining official had never assumed full responsibility for a mining rescue in the past.

Taking direct control, Golborne decided to initiate a plan to drill five-inch bore holes to locate the miners. The miners' precise location was unknown, and such drilling normally required a tolerance for a seven-degree variance in alignment, more than enough to miss the miners' refuge even if its location had been pinpointed. Though he had trained as an engineer before going into retail, Golborne quickly saw that the engineering challenges inherent in the rescue attempts went far beyond his own proficiencies. "I realized that in the technical issues we did not have the needed leadership," he confessed. "I could not provide that leadership. Although I am an engineer, I do not have any technical knowledge about mining."

With volunteers flooding onto the site—some 20 organizations were soon offering their services—a range of other rescue proposals began to emerge. To cope with the flow, Golborne set out to assemble a band of specialists, starting with an experienced engineer from Chile's state-owned copper company who brought both the know-how and credibility required. "There were too many voices," Golborne complained, "and nobody at the site seemed to have the leverage to cut the cake." When the specialist arrived at the San José site, Golborne was unequivocal about the role that the engineer must play: "You have to take charge!"

Working with the miners' families became a separate challenge, as they forcefully pressed for regular updates and, above all, speedy extraction. "We're not going to abandon this camp," declared one of their spokespersons, "until we go out with the last miner left!" Their skepticism ran deep, and emotions ran high. Banners proclaiming "Daddy, we are waiting for you" and "Son, we are here" waved over the families' camp. To another specialist, a psychologist and safety director for one of the state-owned mines, Golborne gave responsibility for working with both the miners' relatives and the many organizations that had arrived to assist.

The government itself was a separate and problematic constituency. Many officials questioned the wisdom of committing the state to an effort that could well end in great tragedy. The mine's owners would bear most of the onus for a disastrous outcome if Golborne did not become engaged, but once he had committed, the state would inevitably share or even take the bulk of the blame. To overcome the lingering risk aversion among Santiago officials, and also to mobilize the government to secure counsel and equipment from around the world, Golborne handed the assignment off to a well-connected insider, the cabinet chief for Chile's Ministry of the Interior.

Further consolidating his team, Golborne removed the mine's owner from any role in the rescue. And he worked to ensure both personal equanimity and single-minded-ness among the small band of leaders he had formed—equanimity because of the intense demands, riveting focus because of the human stakes. But with his top team in place, he then faced a decision on his own decision making: Should he take a role in the life-and-death decisions ahead, or should he leave them to the experts on his team? He worried that the decisions could go wrong without his involvement, but he also feared reactions if he made the final decisions but the rescue later faltered or failed. He feared others would later ask why he had gotten in the middle of it if he knew so little about engineering.

Golborne decided to fall back on the management methods that had served his business well in the past. He asked for guidance and the rationale for technical proposals coming from his team but did not shrink from direct engagement in their final resolution. "I did what I normally do," he explained, and that was to "let the experts talk." And he made sure that his direct reports had compelling reasons for their strategies before they executed them. "With my style," he said, "I started asking questions," but he reserved for himself the final authority for making the decisions.

Underscoring and heightening all of Golborne's actions was the race against time. He assumed that any of the miners who survived the cave-in would have virtually no food, and he worried about life-threatening injuries among those who had not perished. The mining minister accordingly adopted a strategy of redundancy, seeking to reach and then extract the miners through simultaneous parallel measures. The drilling began with no fewer than 10 5-inch bore holes down to locate the miners, and one finally paid off: 15 days after the cave-in, a drill pierced the small cavity where the miners had taken refuge. When the drill head was withdrawn to the surface, taped to it was a message in red letters, "Estamos Bien En El Refugio los 33" (We are fine in the shelter, the 33). For families, it was a moment of jubilation; for Golborne, a personal epiphany and turning point.

Golborne and his team immediately focused on the obvious next task, extracting the miners. They had already vetted some 10 different extraction plans, and their attention converged on three that would open man-sized shafts all the way to the miners' refuge. Each entailed a different approach, and since it was still a race against the clock, Golborne authorized all three to proceed at the same time.

Thirty-three days later, one of three plans, viewed skeptically by some of the engineers at the outset, succeeded before the others. One by one, the miners were transported to the surface in a thin, cable-drawn capsule, and on October

13, the shift supervisor—the last of the miners to be raised—emerged to greet his son and report to the Chilean president, who had joined Golborne for the crowning moment: "I've delivered to you this shift of workers, as we agreed I would."

President Piñera replied, "I gladly receive your shift because you completed your duty, leaving last like a good captain," adding, "You are not the same after this, and Chile won't be the same either." A group of rescuers who were still in the refuge after the last miner ascended displayed a sign seen by millions of television viewers around the world: "Misión Cumplida Chile."

The rescue required that Golborne use virtually all of the Leader's Checklist principles identified so far. He thought strategically, conveyed his character, honored the room, motivated the troops, embraced the front lines, and critically took charge even without a formal brief to do so because he had the management experience to handle the job and was optimally positioned for the task.

Like the disastrous AIG experience, though, the victorious Chilean one also points to still another Leader's Checklist principle: the value of building a top team diverse in capabilities and experience.

---

14. Build a Diverse Top Team: Leaders need to take final responsibility, but leadership is also a team sport best played with an able roster of those collectively capable of resolving all the key challenges.

Maintaining the Leader's Checklist

Organizational leadership has its greatest impact in times of uncertainty and change. When markets are predictable, when change is not in the offing, leaders can coast, at least for a while. It is when uncertainty becomes the norm and turbulence more commonplace that a Leader's Checklist becomes most consequential—a time, that is, much like the present.[36]

To prepare for such moments, we have thus far culled core leadership principles from informed observers, academic researchers, development programs, leaders' assessments, and program participants. In the process, we have discovered a vital skill set that cuts across all sources—capacities such as thinking strategically, acting decisively, and communicating persuasively. Armed with these core precepts, we have also seen how customized principles are essential for leading specific organizations, playing distinct roles within them, running firms in diverse national settings, and facing varying market conditions. Leadership of Indian companies, for example, requires greater emphasis on broad mission and social purpose than is common in the West. Finally, we looked at the need to customize the Leader's Checklist around an individual's immediate world. For a soldier in Iraq, additional principles are required that are distinct from those essential for a salesperson at Microsoft or a firefighter in New York.

With the creation of both core and mission-specific checklists, systematic testing and frequent revision are the essential next steps. In the case of one financial services corporation, for instance, many of the leadership principles that its senior bankers thought vital proved to have little impact when carefully studied—but a small subset did, in fact, result in measurable leadership impact.

Appreciating the value of a Leader's Checklist is, of course, no guarantee that the list will be applied. To close the critical knowing- doing gap, six learning avenues have proven valuable: self-directed study of leadership moments, coaching and mentoring, stretch experiences, after-action review of personal leadership moments, experience with extremely stressful leadership moments, and observing the leadership moments of others. By engaging in this multi-pronged approach, individuals will be more ready to apply their own Leader's Checklist at moments of uncertainty and change.

To be most sustainable, however, a Leader's Checklist needs to be dynamic and adaptable, not static or fixed— constantly updated to reflect new situations and accumulated experience. With repeated study of experiences such as AIG's failure and the successful Chilean rescue operation, a Leader's Checklist should become progressively more grounded in evidence and more complete in coverage.

A checklist for leaders is certainly no substitute for comprehension and judgment, any more than the pilot's or surgeon's checklist is for flying a plane or operating on a patient successfully. The Leader's Checklist is meant to simply be a trigger, and for that purpose, simplicity is essential, as is completeness. Application depends entirely upon the owner's commitment to generate and then use the checklist at a time when it will make a difference. Knowing what a difference checklist principles can make should be all the incentive necessary to assure their deployment. ■

The 15th Principle

Throughout this volume, I have stressed that most of the core principles presented here are applicable in most situations. There is, however, a 15th principle, applicable in all circumstances—a precept for action without which no Leader's Checklist should be considered complete.

Let's revisit a scene from the beginning of this volume, but before we get there, we will need to set the clock back to April 12, 1861. At 4:30 that morning, rebel forces in South Carolina opened fire on a federal fort in Charleston Harbor. The garrison commander gave up the fortress with no fatalities, and though a minor clash compared with what would follow, that opening salvo on Fort Sumter triggered a four-year civil war that would leave more than 620,000 dead.[37]

On both sides, hundreds of thousands stepped forward to serve their cause, including a Maine resident and Bowdoin College professor named Joshua Lawrence Chamberlain. Rising from lieutenant colonel to major general, he would see combat at the battles of Fredericksburg, Gettysburg, and Petersburg, and he was with the Union Army of the Potomac when Robert E. Lee's Army of North Virginia surrendered to the Union Army at Appomattox, Virginia, on April 9, 1865.

To mark the moment, General Ulysses S. Grant, who had accepted the formal surrender on behalf of the Union, ordered a follow-up ceremony for April 12, with more than 4,000 Union soldiers to be lined up at attention on one side of a field. Lee's defeated infantry units were then to march onto the field to place their regimental flags and firearms at the foot of a Union officer in charge. For the honor of orchestrating the event and taking charge of it, Grant designated Chamberlain.

As the first Confederate brigade approached Union forces at the field on April 12, four years to the date since the Rebel firing on Fort Sumter, Chamberlain ordered a bugle call that told Union soldiers to "carry arms"—a posture of respect in which soldiers hold the musket in their right hand with the muzzle perpendicular to their shoulders. Both Union and Confederate soldiers understood its meaning, since their military traditions had emanated from the same sources.

A Southern general riding near the front of the Confederate forces, John B. Gordon, appreciated the respectful signal that Chamberlain's soldiers displayed toward the Rebel soldiers on their day of ignominy, and Gordon ordered the same posture to be returned by his own troops. As described by Chamberlain himself, "Gordon, at the head of the marching column, riding with heavy spirit and downcast face, catches the sound of the shifting arms, looks up, and, taking the meaning," instructed "his successive brigades to pass us with the same position."[38]

The incident became known as a "salute returning a salute," a moment remembered for years by those who witnessed or heard of it, and one that implied reconciliation. Some of Chamberlain's fellow officers were angered by witnessing such a fraternal act after fighting the same soldiers on so many killing fields. And for Chamberlain himself, it was a matter of saluting those who had tried to kill him only two weeks earlier. In a skirmish on March 29, Confederate soldiers had wounded Chamberlain in the arm and chest. A year before that, they shot him through the hip and groin during the Union siege of Petersburg. In all, through 20 battles and numerous skirmishes during three years of service, Chamberlain had been wounded six times and would eventually succumb to the Petersburg injury.[39]

For President Abraham Lincoln, the South's capitulation at Appomattox constituted not only an ending point for the armed rebellion but also a starting point for national reconciliation. Even for him, however, the road to reunification was a bitter pill given the Union's grievous losses on the battlefields. Events would take a horrible personal turn just two days after Chamberlain's salute to the Rebel army as the president and his wife watched a performance at Ford's Theatre in Washington.

For both sides, though, gestures of reconciliation were more important than the hostilities that remained. The latter were natural, the former learned, and Chamberlain's moment at the conclusion of the Civil War serves to remind us of the vital importance of a final Leader's Checklist principle: placing common mission ahead of personal interest or animosity, especially when its seems least natural to do so. This last checklist precept is expressed in our oft-used phrases of "servant" or "selfless" leadership, and it is well captured in a U.S. Marine Corps dictum: "The officer eats last." In business, it appears in Jim Collins's appraisal as one of the defining qualities of those who lead their companies from "good to great."[40] And thus the 15th, final, and most vital of all leadership principles:

---

15. Place Common Interest First. In setting strategy, communicating vision, and reaching decisions, common purpose comes first, personal self-interest last.

This 15th principle could also be heard in the White House on November 16, 2010, when President Barack Obama presented the Medal of Honor to Army Staff Sergeant Salvatore A. Giunta. During the sergeant's second combat tour in Afghanistan, his team had been ambushed by a well-armed insurgent group. Giunta had raced forward under fire at great risk to himself to render aid to the wounded and to rescue an injured GI being dragged away by insurgents. The United States cited Giunta for his "unwavering courage, selflessness, and decisive leadership while under extreme enemy fire" and for his "extraordinary heroism and selflessness above and beyond the call of duty." When the president detailed this selfless act of leadership during the White House ceremony—with Giunta's wife and parents and the survivors of his unit present and the Medal of Honor recipient himself standing at the president's side—the East Room, according to one reporter, "was so silent you could hear a rustle from across the room."[41] ∎

The Owner's Manual

The Leader's Checklist is meant to serve as a trigger to leadership action. Individually, though, each principle should generate a set of questions that will help leaders test, retest, refine, and update their preparedness for almost any situation. Here are sample prompts for each of the precepts:

1. Articulate a Vision.
- Do my direct reports see the forest, not just the trees?
- Does everyone in the firm know not only where we are going, but why?
- Is the destination compelling and appealing?

2. Think and Act Strategically.
- Do we have a realistic plan both for creating short-term results and for mapping out the future?
- Have we considered all the players and anticipated every roadblock?
- Has everybody embraced—and can everybody explain—the firm's competitive strategy and value drivers?

3. **Honor the Room.**
   - Do those in the room know that you respect and value their talents and efforts?
   - Have you made it clear that their upward guidance is always sought?
   - Is there a sense of engagement on the front lines, and do they see themselves as "us," not "them"?

4. **Take Charge.**
   - Are you prepared to take charge even when you are not in charge?
   - If so, do you come with the capacity and position to embrace responsibility?
   - For the technical decisions ahead, are you ready to delegate but not abdicate?

5. **Act Decisively.**
   - Are most of your decisions both good and timely?
   - Do you convey your strategic intent and then let others reach their own decisions?
   - Is your own decision threshold close to a "70-percent" go point?

6. **Communicate Persuasively.**
   - Are the messages about vision, strategy, and character crystal-clear and indelible?
   - Have you mobilized all communication channels, from purely personal to social media?
   - Can you deliver a compelling speech before the elevator passes the 10th floor?

7. Motivate the Troops.
- Have you identified each person's "hot button" and focused on it?
- Do you work personal pride and shared purpose into most communications?
- Are you keeping some ammunition dry for those urgent moments when you need it?

8. Embrace the Front Lines.
- Have you made your intent clear and empowered those around you to act?
- Do you regularly meet with those in direct contact with customers?
- Is everybody able to communicate their ideas and concerns to you?

9. Build Leadership in Others.
- Are all managers expected to build leadership among their subordinates?
- Does the company culture foster the effective exercise of leadership?
- Are leadership development opportunities available to most, if not all, managers?

10. Manage Relations.
- Is the hierarchy reduced to a minimum, and does bad news travel up?
- Are managers self-aware and empathetic?
- Are autocratic, egocentric, and irritable behaviors censured?

11. **Identify Personal Implications.**
    - Do employees appreciate how the firm's vision and strategy impact them individually?
    - What private sacrifices will be necessary for achieving the common cause?
    - How will the plan affect people's personal livelihood and quality of work life?

12. **Convey Your Character.**
    - Have you communicated your commitment to performance with integrity?
    - Do those in the organization know you as a person, and do they know your aspirations and your hopes?
    - Have you been in the same room with everybody who works with you within the past year?

13. **Dampen Over-Optimism.**
    - Have you prepared the organization for unlikely but extremely consequential events?
    - Do you celebrate success but also guard against the by-product of excess confidence?
    - Have you paved the way not only for quarterly results but for long-term performance?

14. **Build a Diverse Top Team.**
    - Have you drawn quality performers into your inner circle?
    - Are they diverse in expertise but united in purpose?
    - Are they as engaged and energized as you?

15. Place Common Interest First.
- In all decisions, have you placed shared purpose ahead of private gain?
- Do the firm's vision and strategy embody the organization's mission?
- Are you thinking like a president or chief executive even if you are not one?

Not all the questions are applicable to every situation, but it is the questioning that counts—as a goad to implementation, whether you are facing a typical day at the office, walking into an off-site event, or in the field with an emergent crisis. ■

Part Two
Leadership in Action

Chilean Minister of Mines Laurence Golborne (right) with
André Sougarret, his chief engineer during the rescue, 2010 (© Corbis)

Rescue of the 33 Miners
An Interview with
Chile's Mining Minister
Laurence Golborne

After a career managing a large retail company in Chile, Laurence Golborne became Minister of Mining under the new Chilean government of President Sebastián Piñera on March 11, 2010. Disaster struck a private mine in the northern Atacama desert on August 5, and Golborne flew to the mine and soon took charge of rescuing the 33 miners trapped more than 2,000 feet below. On October 13, Golborne's crew pulled the last of the trapped miners to the surface in a rescue watched by 1 billion viewers worldwide. I talked with Minister Golborne on June 22, 2011, about his leadership of the miners' rescue and the implications for all who decide to make a difference in the lives of others when they are capable of doing so.

Michael Useem: Laurence, it is our genuine privilege to have you here, coming up all the way from Santiago. We are going to talk about the events of last year. You have a background as an engineer. You ran Chile's largest retail company. On March 11, 2010, you became the Minister of Mining under the new president, Sebastián Piñera. On

August 5th, you were traveling in Ecuador, and you were in the capital, Quito. Around 11:00 PM, your smartphone lit up, and it said, "Mining cave-in, Copiapó; 33 miners." Let's just pick up on that moment. When you saw that on your smartphone, what thoughts ran through your mind? Take us from that moment through August 7th when you arrived at the San José mine around 3:30 in the morning.

Laurence Golborne: To be completely honest, when I received that message, I did not realize how important it was. There are accidents all the time in the mining sector, and we were following all of them. Initially, I thought that it was another one. I was set for that. I asked my under-secretary to go there and to find out what was going on. During that night, I received different information. I received the information that there were a large number of people trapped, 30-something. We didn't know, really, how many at that time.

I talked to the president, and I said, "We have this issue." We thought initially that the miners were dead, [as is often the case] when you have these kinds of collapses.... The president told me, "Well, it is better if you go back to Chile. That is the reality." When I arrived there, after traveling all of Friday from Quito to Lima, then Lima to Santiago, and then from Santiago to Copiapó, I arrived at the mine on Saturday, the 7th, around 2:00 or 3:00 AM.

Then I saw the human drama. At that moment, all the families were there. They were filled with angst, and there was no trust. There was no information. Nobody really knew what was going on. The company that was managing this situation and responsible for this was trying to organize the issues. A lot of volunteers and other mining companies sent rescue teams to help in this process, trying to organize this issue. But the main problem was with the families. They were really upset and sad. Mainly, they didn't trust that anybody could help them, and they were afraid that the company and the government were lying to them. I had to start to try to establish a relationship based on trust with them.

Initially, we were trying to avoid the responsibility of the whole operation. Because, according to our legislation, we have no right to interfere in that process. But after 24 hours, we saw that it was impossible. After we had a lot of problems that Saturday, President Piñera decided to come back to Chile. He went to the mine, and he met some of the relatives of the families. We chose a small group of them. To face 300 or 400 people who were in the middle of such suffering was too complicated. President Piñera committed that we would, with all our effort, find them. At that moment, I felt empowered to take control.

Useem: That was a big decision, a life-defining decision. What were some of the downsides that went into your own thinking at the time as you thought about the risk entailed in the Republic of Chile taking full responsibility for rescuing the 33 miners still not found, when it was not even clear if they were injured or alive?

Golborne: Yeah, this is what I normally highlight most. The political decision that President Piñera made was key in this. I have never seen, in any other disaster in the world, a government that became as bold as we did in this case. I cannot explain why President Piñera made this decision. But that was key for the success of this operation. Politically speaking, it wasn't something advisable to do. I remember when he was traveling to Chile, I said, "Don't come here. Go directly to Santiago. I will keep you informed about what is going on here. But don't come here because you are going to get personally involved in this." But he put people's lives [as a top priority], and he decided to do it. And that was, as I said, key for the success of this story.

Useem: Let's take the chronology forward. You're there early on August 7th. Your first concern, of course, is to find the miners. The mining shaft is impossible to enter, way too dangerous for a rescue crew, and much of it is blocked anyway. You set about trying to find them by sinking a five-inch shaft down the 2,000 feet or so to where you thought they were. It is a very famous moment now: On August 22, a drill head came back to the surface with a note on it, "We are the 33. We're in a refuge, and we're fine." What was your reaction when you saw that note?

Golborne: It was one of the best moments in my life. I cannot express what we felt. In some video footage, you can see we really had a state of grace, a sort of epiphany. We had broken that morning early, around 6:00, [due to a faint tapping sound]. We tried to listen: [It sounded like] something hitting the pipes with hammers. I remember I called President Piñera around 8:00 AM and said, "President, I am listening to something. I cannot assure you that there is anybody alive. Maybe it is my imagination. Maybe it is water that is falling or rocks that are falling inside the pipe. But I am listening to something."

We spent six hours trying to calm down the people while the machine was taking out the bars. This is a machine that has 600 meters of bars, and you have to take them out. And first, we saw the hammer of the last bar painted in red. That was the first moment of emotion that we had. Because the moment that we saw it, one of the operators says, "Minister, it's painted in red." I said, "Well, are you sure that it wasn't painted before?" I used that Chile-ism to talk to this guy at that moment. "No, boss, I am sure that it wasn't." So we knew that somebody was alive.

Then we found a yellow bag tied to the head of the hammer with a letter inside—a letter from Mario Gomez to his wife, Lilianette—and we started reading it. While we were doing that, someone looked inside the hammer head and found a piece of paper that said, "We are okay, the 33." We had a protocol for communicating to families, but at the moment that we got that paper, everything was forgotten. Some people ran down to where the families were, telling them they were alive. We were just yelling and really, really happy.

Useem: A fantastic moment, although it is the end of the beginning. The miners are over 2,000 feet below. The hardness of the rock is described as being twice that of granite. You can't get to them through the shaft. You have to devise a plan now. It is in your hands. You have taken charge when you were not initially in charge. As you move from August 22 to now creating a big enough shaft to bring people up, it's a challenge. You are an engineer by background. But you had been in retail as a manager, a very large retail company. You served as chief executive. Please talk about how you thought about your team, who you wanted on the team, and ultimately, how you got the team to be a wonderfully high-performing, time-driven team that brought up the miners not too many days later.

Golborne: Well, I will start with the last part of the question. Normally, when you are managing any group of people, what you need to do is to try to sell them a dream, to try to commit them behind an objective that they have to be very tight on. In this case, that wasn't necessary. Everybody was so committed to this task, that from the first day, everyone gave all their effort for the success of this task. People were very motivated. During the first 17 days, and after we had failure after failure, obviously, people got disappointed. And this enthusiasm diminished. That is a role that you have to maintain to try to keep people committed.

I was very concerned about what we would have done after 30 or 45 days, because that situation would have been more complicated from a commitment point of view. But we had very committed people. What we did is to try to organize this as any task that you face, to separate different teams into different tasks. We created a group of people who were involved in all of the family matters. By families, I mean people who are the relatives of the miners, to try to help them with their problems—very common problems, including what to do with children…. In addition, we were in the middle of a desert, [without resources] to support a real city that we were creating with 2,000–3,000 people living there. At the peak, we had more than 2,000 people living or going there. We had to deal with all those kinds of things and with the health problems of the miners and the families, and also, the technical issues.

We created two groups to handle the technical issues. One was working inside the mine, trying to do the rescue, doing the drillings, and dealing with those kinds of things. But we also create a second team in Santiago, in the capital city, dealing with different technologies to design how we could rescue and the best technologies to keep these people alive if we found them, and how to get them out in that case, too.

When we finally found them, we had all these plans already designed. We just started with them. But, as in normal life, the plan that finally succeeded wasn't the one that was designed initially. It was designed by the people who were working on site. They did a great job. I think those guys are the real heroes of this process.

Useem: As the rescue went forward in that fashion, I think you had plans with letters to designate them A through F. As I recall, it was Plan B that finally did reach the miners. In all those very technical decisions—which plan would work best, which plan should you follow, what would happen as the plans unfold—to what extent did you take an active role in those technical decisions? At what point did you opt to leave those decisions to others?

Golborne: We created a team there. We worked together, all of us. Obviously, there were specialists. They had the knowledge to give us the right technical support. But the decisions were made essentially on a collective basis. We discussed it with André Sougarret, Felipe Mathews, and other people who were working there. When a decision needed to be made, the political responsibilities for the whole operation was mine. So I had to make the decision.

But I remember, at the end, we had a lot of discussion regarding the casing of the hole. I met with eight geologists. I started asking the opinion of each of them. I had my own opinion when I entered that room. But I wanted to have their feedback and to try to see the decision that I was making was the proper one. Finally, we decided not to case the whole hole, and 50 meters at the beginning. And it ended up being a good decision. But we tried to make the decision as a group. When there was a different position, I had to make the final one.

Useem: A final question for you. On October 12th and October 13th, the miners began to come up finally, one after another. It is estimated that 1 billion people worldwide watched at least one of those miners come to the surface. It is one of the miraculous events of last year. Looking back on that, and thinking about what you learned about leadership, what lessons stand out?

Golborne: Well, maybe the most important one is: Never give up. When you think that you have to jump a channel, a river, whatever, and you think that you are not going to be able to do it, probably you are going to fail. So you have to be positive. You have to be optimistic. You have to think that it will be possible. No matter how hard the task looks, you need to feel that you are able to do it. In that group, nobody at any time gave up. I think that is key. A leader of a group needs to be an example for that.

Also, you need to try to be on the field, to be with the guys. That means, with the people who were operating the machines, with the families, the relatives of the miners, and the technical people. They need to feel that you are committed to them and the job that they are doing. And I tried to do that. I spent my days there, working and planning. But also, talking with people, talking with the families, knowing how they were, the fears and the problems, if everything was okay, listening to people who suggest things, to be open to different ideas.

And also, I always gave myself some time to go to machine after each machine, saying hello to the guys who were working there for 8, 12, or more hours drilling, to say, "Thank you. We are going to do it. Go ahead." That signal gives them a sense of commitment and importance in what they were doing. I think that is very important to try to motivate people. You need to do all of this on top of the technical stuff. You need to have competent people. You need to have people who know what they are doing. And to leave them to work outside of the pressure. That is something that I tried to do, too, to not allow the pressure we had from the media, from the families, to pass through our shield to affect the people who were working. Because they had enough problems trying to solve the technical issues than to try to deal with other issues that are emotional and complicated.

Useem: Laurence, thank you for joining us. As Minister of Mines and now also Minister of Energy, we are extremely appreciative of having time with you. Thank you for taking charge when you were not in charge last October, making an enormous difference for the 33 families of the miners trapped, but maybe equally, helping the world appreciate what it takes to lead in a situation that is time-driven, time-constrained, and the stakes are very high. The way forward was not obvious. You brought the miners up. We thank you for that.

Golborne: Well, thank you very much for inviting me. I think what I face, what we faced at that moment, was something that everybody, on a daily basis, faces in their own life. You never know what is going to happen tomorrow. Problems could be smaller or larger, but the issue is the same. You always have to face them with faith that you are going to be able to solve it. ■

New York City Fire Department's Joseph Pfeifer at 9:59 a.m. on September 11, 2001, when the South Tower collapsed, as captured in a screenshot image from the documentary 9/11. (© Goldfish Pictures)

Leading on 9/11 and Beyond

An interview with New York Fire Department Chief Joseph Pfeifer

Joseph Pfeifer joined the New York City Fire Department in 1981, and by 2001, he had become a Battalion Chief, responsible for commanding major incidents. On the morning of September 11, 2001, he was on a routine call near the World Trade Center when disaster struck. Seeing the first aircraft hit the North Tower, he rushed to the scene and radioed the alarm, the first FDNY Fire Chief to take command. Today he is New York City Fire Department's Chief of Counterterrorism and Emergency Preparedness and a Citywide Command Chief. I talked with Chief Pfeifer on August 15, 2011, about his leadership of the 9/11 rescue efforts and the leadership lessons from a career of public service for those who are also called to place their own leadership on the line.

Michael Useem: Joe, it is great to have you here. I am going to begin by asking you about your career with the New York City Fire Department, which you joined in 1981.

What have been some of the most formative experiences that helped you learn how to lead people?

Joseph Pfeifer: When I first came into the fire department as a probationary firefighter, I was told the most important thing is to know the job, to know what you need to do. So, I started reading the fire manuals and procedures. But that is only half of it. The other part is actually experiencing firefighting, which provides a tacit knowledge of how to force a door or how to climb an aerial ladder 100 feet in the air. But to be a good firefighter, to be good at anything, is really having the competency in knowing what to do.

As I became an officer, it was more than just knowing what to do, it became being responsible for firefighters. That point was made after 9/11, actually. I was in command of a third-alarm fire up in the Bronx. We had about 100 firefighters at the scene and about three dozen pieces of apparatus. When the fire goes out, I'm leaving and I have this firefighter running down the block after me. He calls, "Chief, chief, chief!" I stop and I turn around, and he says, "Chief, I just want to let you know that I'll follow you down any hallway." Now, for a firefighter, the most dangerous part is a hallway: It becomes like a chimney, and all the smoke and heat fills the hallway. I thought, Wow, this is a very nice compliment.

Then, when I got back to my car, I realized he was saying more than "I'll follow you." He was saying, "I'll be with you, I'll follow you, and I want you to keep us safe." See, leadership is not about giving orders; it's about sharing the danger. That firefighter was saying that because of what I have done in the past, he'll follow me, he'll be with me during the next major event. That is an awesome responsibility. I could actually feel the pressure of the responsibility for others. And he meant what he said.

Useem: A formative moment.

Pfeifer: Very much so.

Useem: Joe, let me ask about a set of documents that I know you helped prepare, a set of checklists for the New York Fire Department. You have a checklist if there's a radio-activity release. You have a checklist in case of a building collapse. You have a checklist called the Mayday checklist. Talk about why you developed these checklists and then about how they are used in practice by members of the New York Fire Department.

Pfeifer: We use checklists as shortcuts. For a radiological incident, we don't handle that frequently, so we need a list of procedures to follow. During a fire, as the fire becomes more and more complex and we have to make decisions, the stress level increases. One of the most difficult times as a commanding chief would be a Mayday. Mayday is a message from a firefighter that the firefighter is in trouble: the firefighter is trapped or doesn't know his or her way out of the building. Something is seriously wrong, a life-or-death situation. Immediately the stress level goes up, and you have to deal with that, and at the same time, fight the fire. So, we use a checklist and an acronym. The word we use is LUNAR. What we want to know is the member's location, his or her unit, the person's name, the assignment, and what resources we have available. That is critical information, so we can make sure that firefighter gets out of the building alive. It helps to know what to do right away, and it is very focused.

Another thing we are dealing with now is how to use technology as a checklist. For example, we are developing an electronic command board, or what I like to call a command pad, which is very similar to the iPad. We are able to see where our units are deployed within a building structure. One of the important things for safety is to do searches of every floor where there is fire, and even floors where there is no fire. We are required to do that within 15 minutes. As a checklist, we use visual cues. If the search is not completed within 15 minutes, the floor will turn red on the command pad. Instantly, that's a cue to the incident commander to check on the statuses with searchers.

If we do a primary search, it turns yellow. If we do secondary search afterward, it turns green. We use the intuitive knowledge of a stoplight—red, yellow, green—to give the incident commander the same cues as a checklist, but now we are doing it in a visual format.

Useem: Looking at the Mayday checklist, it looked to me as if you have a good number of items, all of which are pretty mission critical, and you probably want your officers to get through all of the items. One in particular caught my attention, having gone through your training program with seven of my colleagues a few months ago. The Mayday command is part of the checklist protocol. If you're a trapped firefighter and you say "Mayday," you have to repeat it three times. Why is that important?

Pfeifer: It is important because we are dealing with wireless communications. We are dealing with radios. We want to make sure that the message comes across. If a firefighter is in trouble, the firefighter will say, "Mayday, Mayday, Mayday," and then give a message. It helps ensure the message gets through. It also tells the other firefighters to stop talking on the radio and listen. In just three words, a lot is being communicated.

Useem: Speaking of Mayday, as fate would have it, on the morning of 9/11, you were down near the World Trade Center checking on a gas leak. It was a pretty routine day. You did look up a few minutes before 9:00 AM—at 8:46 to be very precise—and you saw the first plane hit the North Tower. You were the ranking commander in proximity to the World Trade Center. You played a very important role in bringing firefighters and emergency service people in there. You were also the incident commander in the North Tower. Just take us from 8:30 on the morning of 9/11, through the next couple of hours.

Pfeifer: On the morning of 9/11, we were checking a gas leak in the street, and it was pretty much a routine emergency for us. Then at 8:46 in the morning, we heard the loud roar of a plane. You never hear a plane going overhead in Manhattan because of the height of the buildings. We saw the plane actually aim and crash into the North Tower. At that moment, we knew we were going to the biggest fire of our lives. I got on the radio, and I gave the message to transmit a second alarm. I told the firefighters I was with to respond in with me.

About a minute later, I had just a little bit of time to think. I gave another message, and very clearly, I transmitted a third alarm for more resources. Then I said to the dispatcher that the plane had aimed for the building. I knew that this was not an accident, that this was a terrorist event. Then I proceeded to give further orders on where I wanted fire-fighters to stage and where I wanted them to go in.

I can remember stepping into the lobby of the World Trade Center's North Tower. It looked like the plane had actually hit the lobby. There was debris all over the place, glass broken, people injured, some people burnt. I went up to the fire safety director, and I was told that the fire was somewhere above the 78th floor. As firefighters came in, I gave an order. The order was to go up, to evacuate people from the building, and to rescue those who couldn't get out by themselves. I told them to go up to the 70th floor. At the time, I figured eight floors was a good measure of safety. We would regroup there, and then try to get people out who were above the fire.

As we were doing that, a little bit before 9:00, we gave the order to evacuate the South Tower. But a few minutes later, at 9:03, we heard another loud roar, and this was the second plane crashing into the South Tower. At that point, we divided our command. There was one commander in the North Tower, one in the South Tower, and our chief of department, the overall person in charge, was across the street. Firefighters came in, and they started to climb. They started to encourage people to come down: "Don't stop. Keep going down. Keep moving down. Get out of the building."

Then, at 9:59 that morning, we heard the crashing sound. We moved about 20 meters from where we were standing in the lobby to a passageway that led across West Street. The lobby was covered with dust, and it went completely black. Now, for firefighters, being in darkness is not a big deal. We operate in that all the time. But at that moment some of the other chiefs were saying we had to get out of the building, something very important to do. We had to move out. We couldn't command in the lobby; we had to leave. I knew how to get out of the building. See, this was my building. I was there hundreds of times. That bought me some time to think. In that few seconds, I knew that if we couldn't command there, we needed to get the firefighters out also. So I picked up my handy radio, and I said, "Command to all units in Tower 1, evacuate the building!" And the firefighters started to come down.

But being many floors above, it took a long time to come down. What we didn't realize at the time was that we were running out of time. As firefighters came down, they didn't think of just themselves. One lieutenant I can remember stopped around the ninth floor and directed other firefighters to other stairs because the stairs they were coming down would have led to the debris-filled court-yard. Another unit, Ladder Six, stopped and noticed a woman who couldn't continue any longer. They picked her up and started to carry her down.

We made our way out into the street, and standing in front of the World Trade Center, we couldn't tell what had happened. It was covered with dust and debris, and we were never told that an entire 110-story building had just collapsed to the ground. Then, at 10:28 that morning, we heard the crashing and the roar of the North Tower collapsing, and we began to run. But with bunker gear, you can't run that fast or that far. So we crouched down behind a truck, and this beautiful summer morning that was full of sunshine turned completely black. You couldn't see your hand in front of your face. We could hear the steel crashing all around us, and we were just waiting, really, to be crushed because we knew we were too close to the World Trade Center.

Then the noises stopped, and it became silent. There was no more talk on the radio. There was just this eerie sound of total silence. It was like a new snowfall. You just heard nothing. It was just this muffled sound. When we got up and we walked back to the Trade Center, or where the Trade Center had been, we saw only rubble. We couldn't believe that the buildings—the two towers—had just crashed to the ground. On my radio, I heard a call from Ladder Six, "Ladder Six to command, we're trapped in the B stairs on the fourth floor." Well, I looked at the pile, and although I knew the building well, I had no idea where the captain was.

That was the captain who was carrying the woman down. By slowing their descent, they were able to survive in a little pocket. That captain got his unit and the woman out alive, a miraculous story. But there were other stories: that lieutenant for Engine 33 and the 343 firefighters who died. In total, we lost 2,750 people in New York. But amongst the rubble and amongst the pain, we saw glimmers of hope. See, terrorism tries to take away people's hope. But what we saw that day is people helping each other. What we saw in the days and months to follow was the silhouette of a firefighter on the pile at Ground Zero searching to make rescues initially and then to recover those who were lost.

It is important that we don't focus just on the sadness of that day because we did save 20,000 people. And 9/11 is something different, it's not just an event for New York City, or just an event for the United States; it's an international event because no matter where you were in the world, you experienced it through the media, a type of global trauma. But ten years after 9/11, it gives the international community a voice against terrorism—that small roadside bombing, that hotel bombing. It's a united voice, a world voice that says terrorism is wrong. As we look at the tenth 9/11 anniversary, and other anniversaries, it is really an international event that gives all victims of terrorism a voice.

Useem: Joe, I know in the 10 years since 9/11, you have spent a lot of time thinking about that event, including its implications for leadership and for getting through a crisis of that kind. You worked with the 9/11 Commission. You have written about what happened and some of the lessons learned. Please talk about a couple of the leading lessons that you have now worked with since the events of that terrible day.

Pfeifer: I think the 9/11 Commission Report captured it well by saying that there was a lack of information-sharing. Certainly there was a lack of information-sharing with the intelligence community before the events of 9/11. But there was also a lack of information-sharing among emergency responders, the police, and fire department. I think one of the important lessons learned is that during a catastrophic event, during a disaster, we need to share information.

There is also a sense of interdependency. We need to work together.

One of the things that I wrote about is that during any major event, there will always be organizational bias. As the stress of an incident increases, groups turn to their own: firefighters go to firefighters, police go to police, and emergency medical form their own groups. But during a disaster, we need just the opposite. We need for those groups to collaborate. As we look at other major disasters around the world—an earthquake, a tsunami, another terrorist event—it is necessary for groups to come together and communicate and work with each other to deal with the disaster at hand.

Useem: I know you have spent a lot of time building that integration and ability to communicate since then. As you have taken on additional duties now as Chief of Counter-terrorism for the City of New York, what keeps you up at night these days, 10 years after 9/11?

Pfeifer: With my job, there are a lot of things that keep me up at night. One of the things that I worry about the most is a type of an attack that we saw occur a few years ago in Mumbai. As a matter of fact, it is referred to as a Mumbai-style attack, where there are multiple active shooters in different locations using improvised explosive devices and using fire. It's those three weapons—guns, explosives, and fire—that keep me up at night. In combination, they are the most deadly. The World Trade Center was brought down not by the planes, but by fire. We see that terrorists are starting to learn from their own activity. And we also must learn.

For us to battle an event that uses multiple means of weapons, multiple means of attack, we need to work with each other. It's something that worries us in New York. I'm in contact with London, and it worries them. But I think by sharing information within the City of New York and with other cities, we will be better prepared to deal with that type of event, if it does occur.

Useem: Joe, a final question for you. You have been with the New York City Fire Department for 30 years. You were at Ground Zero on 9/11. For the last decade you have thought a lot about how to build out of that to prepare for whatever may happen in the future. These types of catastrophic events have been brought home as we watch what happened with BP in the Gulf, the Fukushima power plants in Japan, the disaster in Haiti with that earthquake. On the basis of your experience with the New York Fire Department, 9/11, and the decade since then, what advice would you have for people who are responsible in the private sector, public sector, and in nonprofit organizations for thinking about how to get through a catastrophic event?

Pfeifer: When we look at those events, we want to think of how to manage it, or as the military refers to it, command and control. We want one person to run the whole thing. And I think we have learned since 9/11, and looking at those major events, that is not what leaders do. Leaders during a catastrophic event do more than just manage the event. They do three other things: they connect, collaborate, and coordinate.

When an event occurs, the first thing that needs to be done is to hastily form networks at the scene of the incident, among firefighters, rescuers, law enforcement, and medical personnel, so they can start to communicate and work together. Away from the incident, we have to connect to those emergency operations centers that we have created and have information passed from, for example, New York City to the state, to the national operations center down in Washington, DC.

Once we have formed these networks, the incident commanders, the people who are responsible for dealing with the event, need to get together and collaborate. So there's this flattening of command, not just one person. Now we have the major decision-makers getting together and figuring out what to do. What they do is coordinate the resources that we need to get a job done. What we are seeing now is that it's not just one resource, it involves multiple resources. For example, during Hurricane Katrina in New Orleans, we had the Coast Guard spot fires. The New Orleans Fire Department, with the assistance of the New York City Fire Department, went out and extinguished the fires. But they also went out with law enforcement for protection. It was that combination and coordination of resources. When we look at leadership during a disaster, whether it is in an emergency response or in business or in nonprofits, it is the combination of what we call C5: command and control, connect, collaborate, and coordinate.

Useem: Joe, on that note, let me thank you for 30 years of service to the City of New York. Let me thank you for putting your leadership and your life on the line on that very fateful morning on 9/11. And thank you for your insights that have come with a decade of reflecting on 9/11 and all the threats that we now face, so that the rest of us can be more prepared to face those calamities that may be out there one day. We need to be ready to do what we have to do if, heaven forbid, we do face another disaster.

Pfeifer: Thank you, Mike. ■

Mission-Critical

An Interview about the Leader's Checklist with the Author

Knowledge@Wharton: Mike, you have written several books on leadership. What was the inspiration for *The Leader's Checklist*?

Michael Useem: I became convinced that everybody needs a leader's checklist by virtue of watching leaders in action who didn't have one. They made—call it "an unforced error," or sometimes a couple of unforced errors. Simply having a piece of paper that says, "Don't forget to honor the room" or "Don't forget to talk about company strategy" would help people avoid these kinds of mistakes. It really goes back to Atul Gawande's great argument in *The Checklist Manifesto*. Most surgeons and most pilots don't make errors. But when they do make an error, it has significant implications. A checklist helps prevent such a mistake.

Knowledge@Wharton: It's catastrophic.

Useem: Yes, catastrophic. Mission critical. And so for that reason, the Federal Aviation Administration (FAA) and military aviation authorities many years ago imposed an aviator's checklist. Hospitals in the United States and abroad have begun to impose the Surgical Safety Checklist, very similar in import. Because even surgeons—who are smart, well-trained and have done a thousand procedures of a given kind—still make an error once in a while, given all the complexity, stress, and fast-moving circumstances they operate under. In surgery, you don't want that to happen. And by implication, you don't want that to happen to a leader who is trying to help everybody understand where the company is going in the coming 12 months but forgets to hit all those items on the checklist.

Knowledge@Wharton: You pick out the Chilean mining disaster and rescue, the near collapse of AIG, and the ceremonial surrender of the Confederate Army during the Civil War as your three main examples to kick you off. Very briefly, why did you pick those three?

Useem: I think it's very important for people to appreciate why a given item is on the checklist and to see where it is illustrated by somebody's leadership moment—or not illustrated, as in the case of AIG. By seeing that, I think we hang on to these ideas. That becomes critical in a leader's checklist, as opposed to an aviator's checklist, in the sense that with a pilot, you can't take off if you don't go through a checklist in modern aircraft. Literally, the aircraft won't go forward if you haven't hit the buttons on the electronic panel.

But in leadership, we have no FAA equivalent. We've got to walk around with this set of ideas ourselves. And my own experience is that people remember, hang on to, and are ready to use some of the ideas of the checklist if those ideas are embedded in something very graphic, something very memorable, something very powerful. And just to recall that AIG went belly-up back on September 16, 2008, partly because the people who led that firm didn't have a full checklist. That serves as a reminder.

Knowledge@Wharton: So these three examples correlate to specific items on your checklist?

Useem: Yes. At the outset of the book, I identify 15 principles.

In the case of AIG, leadership principles were not followed by the CEO of AIG, or by the managing director of AIGFP, the financial products group that led to AIG's downfall. Keep in mind that the leader's calling is to help people stay confident without being over-confident, to be realistic, to guard against hubris. What happened in the case of AIGFP is it began to insure all these fancy products on the premise that AIG, the parent, would keep its Triple-A Standard & Poor's credit rating. That was vital to the way that AIG operated. But credit agencies do have a habit of downgrading organizations.

Think AIG, think Greece at the moment. Neither the AIGFP managing director nor Martin Sullivan, who was AIG's CEO at the time, really had a rainy-day scenario. There were plenty of signs that downgrading was possible after Bear Stearns collapsed. It was in the spring of 2008 that agencies—in part because they're under a lot of criticism—are beginning to downgrade many companies. But AIG's top people evidently had no worst-case scenario:

"Suppose we get downgraded?" And it was that downgrading that put AIG under.

Knowledge@Wharton: So that was their lack of a leadership vision or leadership moment?

Useem: Yes.

Knowledge@Wharton: In terms of the Chilean Minister of Mining, what one principle or two principles do you think were demonstrated in that rescue?

Useem: There were many actions that Chilean Minister of Mining Laurence Golborne took between August and October of 2010 to bring the 33 trapped miners to the surface. One factor, though, in particular that I emphasize is that—given his background in retail, not mining—he didn't bring any technical knowledge of how to mine, let alone how to rescue miners 2,000 feet below. He not only had to get the miners out—that was a huge engineering challenge—he also had to manage relations with the government. There were 2,000 full-time reporters on site with plenty of time to find Golborne and ask him questions. And he had 33 families who had a very strong point of view on just about everything he was doing.

To his credit, he pulled together an extremely diverse team. Leadership is both an individual and a team sport. You can't lead if you don't have a good and diverse team. That was graphically evident back in the Atacama Desert last summer and fall.

Knowledge@Wharton: And what about the Confederate Army having to formally surrender at Appomattox?

Useem: Yes, Robert E. Lee surrendered his army to Union General Ulysses S. Grant, and Grant in turn assigned the organization of a ceremonial surrender three days later to one of his officers, Joshua Lawrence Chamberlain.

Knowledge@Wharton: How was that handled by Chamberlain?

Useem: It was a day of ignominy for Lee's army, the Army of Northern Virginia, 25,000 strong. They surrendered April 9. The "surrender at Appomattox" is the phrase that historians have given us. Meanwhile, though, as Grant signed the document with Lee in a private home, a telegram goes up to Lincoln in Washington. Lincoln, of course, is thrilled. But he also is mindful of what's next.

Knowledge@Wharton: The future of the country now that the war was over.

Useem: Which is reconciliation. And that's a little bit of a bitter pill since, as we know in retrospect, it is just five days before April 14, when the President and Mrs. Lincoln had tickets to Ford's Theatre, where the President was assassinated by John Wilkes Booth.

Lincoln, in the White House, is thinking, "I've got to start the process of reconciliation."

Meanwhile, Grant gives Joshua Lawrence Chamberlain, a one-star non-regular army officer, the almost singular honor of organizing the ceremonial surrender of Lee's army. The formal surrender is all over on April 9. But the ceremonial surrender comes on April 12. Grant says to Chamberlain, "Chamberlain, you're going to be in charge of the informal surrender. You decide what to do. I'm only going to require that you collect the muskets and the flags." So Chamberlain—in a very unorthodox move—brings his own 4,000 Union soldiers to attention with what is called "carry arms." The Confederate officers, about to give over their flags and their arms to Chamberlain and who come out of the same military tradition, know that "carry arms" is a mark of great respect.

Chamberlain, believing that Lincoln probably wants reunification, decides to help reconciliation in his own smaller way. This moment becomes known as the "salute returning the salute." The Confederate commander, John Gordon, who's marching toward the field with the 4,000 Union soldiers all lined up, sees them "carry arms." He says to his own subordinate officers, "carry arms." The two armies saluted each other, and that leads to the 15th point on the Leader's Checklist.

With a foundation of 12 principles, I have added a 13th from AIG, 14th from the miners' rescue in Chilé, and then a 15th from Chamberlain at Appomattox, which is the most important principle of all. It runs through Jim Collins' book *Good to Great*, for example. And that is, at the start of the day and at the end of the day, leadership is not about you; it's not about anything in a leadership position, except the mission and purpose of the organization. Chamberlain is criticized for saluting the enemy, but arguably it was the right gesture given the mission of the moment.

Knowledge@Wharton: Right. So those are three very important principles that you have just illustrated very well. Which of the other 12 are the hardest for a leader to focus on?

Useem: That's an easy question to answer because I've noticed this one missing more often in practice than any of the other 15. I have a phrase I use there to capture it. It's a bit of shorthand: "Honor the room." In a discussion with one person, a team, a class, an off-site meeting, before you get off-stage, take a moment to tell the people you are with—those who may be ready to follow you—that you know who they are, that you respect what they're doing, and that you're extremely grateful for their hard work, upon which you're going to get your job done.

Knowledge@Wharton: You also note in your book that there needs to be customized checklists for distinct times and contexts, including what the company is, what country a business is operating in, what is happening at that moment in time, and so forth. We're experiencing, obviously, the tail end of a recession and a very struggling economy. What would your checklist be for companies trying to get out of that recession and recover?

Useem: There are different ways to answer the question. The way I've chosen to answer it in this particular book is to draw upon the thinking of 14 people we interviewed right in the middle of the height of the financial crisis of 2008 and 2009. We went to 14 CEOs and asked them a very simple question: "Look, in light of what you are in the middle of now, what are you doing a little bit differently from what you ordinarily would have done?" The one thing that really stands out—from among six actions that were somewhat distinctive and really should be seen as add-ons to the checklist—is the cardinal importance of being clear about what's out there, saying what, in your realistic appraisal of the environment, is the good news and what sometimes is the very bad news. And repeatedly communicating an extremely realistic appraisal, along with an unequivocal recommitment to what you're trying to do, the purpose and goals of the enterprise.

Something like: "Don't forget that this is why we're on earth, this is our mission, it seems like hard times, here's how hard it is—but we're going to get through it."

Knowledge@Wharton: Can you name a few of those CEOs who were among the 14?

Useem: We interviewed A.G. Lafley of P&G, for example, and Ed Breen, who essentially came in and rebuilt Tyco, cleaned up the mess in one of the most remarkable remakes of all time.

Knowledge@Wharton: When you were researching your book, was there anything that surprised you? You have studied leadership for quite a while, so you must have seen and heard it all. But was there something that was surprising or that was so counter-intuitive that you were shocked by it?

Useem: Here's the most counter-intuitive point of all, which has nothing to do with leadership, but it has implications for it. Several articles published this year in the *New England Journal of Medicine* compare hospitals that use surgeons' checklists with those that don't. You had to be careful—different kinds of patients and different kinds of protocols all had to be taken into account. A hospital that does not use a surgeon's checklist has, on average, a rate of mortality of about one percent. But at hospitals that use a surgeon's checklist, required and enforced by the surgeon and sometimes the chief nurse in the room, mortality rates are cut in half.

Knowledge@Wharton: A half of one percent?

Useem: Yes. Not a big deal, unless that happens to be your daughter or son who is in that 50 basis-point range.

Knowledge@Wharton: Absolutely.

Useem: I'm actually surprised the reduction was that large. And, by implication, in a study yet to be done, my guess is that a leader who gets out there, pretty consistently applying the 15 most important principles, is going to be materially better for it. I can't prove that now, although intuitively, it seems right. I think that was the most surprising element. That it really does make a difference, especially among seasoned professionals.

Knowledge@Wharton: That raises the question of what proof can you have or can you fall back on to show that the checklist makes a difference. It's fairly subjective and almost anecdotal—or maybe not. Comparing one hospital to another hospital is a little bit easier than saying this list makes a certain leader into a better one, maybe by saving people's jobs, or whatever.

Useem: It's an amalgam of sources of evidence. To cite one well-known method, Jim Collins in *Good to Great* takes 11 companies that went from good to great and 11 companies that did not, over five years. What's the difference? One that emerges is that the CEOs of those 11 companies that went from good to great were totally focused on mission and absolutely not focused on their own welfare or getting ahead. There are lots of particular studies out there that get at this facet or that facet, but no study that I know of—and I haven't done it myself—has taken all 15 of these separate items. Yet pulling from a range of sources, I've become convinced that these 15 are all mission critical. Which means that you've got to have them all. None is sufficient.

Let's take the number one item—having a vision, a strategy, and being able to execute around it. I will track down a study that finds that chief executives who are more strategic and more thoughtful about vision do perform more strongly. What I don't have though—it's a good challenge—are those involving all 15.

Knowledge@Wharton: If you could name, without any explanation, the top four leaders who are actively leading today, who would they be?

Useem: Indra Nooyi of Pepsi. Steve Jobs at Apple. I am drawn to Laurence Golborne, and I have long-standing and continuing great admiration for the man who built Lenovo,

Liu Chuanzhi. I picked the four in part because they each illustrate a different part of the spectrum there.

Knowledge@Wharton: I notice, of course, that one of them is a woman. Did you find any traits or principles that you think are actually more likely to resonate with leaders who are women than with leaders who are men?

Useem: You know, from a research standpoint, no, and even intuitively, no, in observing leaders like Indra Nooyi or Ellen Kullman, who has a very good start in taking over as CEO of DuPont.

Knowledge@Wharton: It's good if we're beyond the point where we have to say "women are different from men in terms of leadership."

Useem: Yes, that's where I am. To make an obvious point, there is more variation within gender than between gender these days. To put that differently—I think men and women can learn from Indra Nooyi and Ellen Kullman and Laurence Golborne.

Knowledge@Wharton: You note in the beginning of your book that the "animating premise" of *The Leader's Checklist* is that effective leadership can be learned, and indeed, should be learned. Does this mean that you're negating the role of gut reaction or spontaneous reaction to events? Can people still be leaders by the seat of their pants, if you know what I'm getting at?

Useem: There is a lot of research evidence on that. A great argument comes from Malcolm Gladwell, the author of the book called *Blink*. He says intuition is extremely important and vital to have. Gut instinct is a great platform for making good and timely decisions. Having said that, gut instinct, intuition that is not informed by experience, is likely to be a disaster. So when the author of *Blink* writes as a subtitle, *The Power of Thinking Without Thinking*, the sub-subtitle should be, *After Having Digested Prior Experience*. And there's just lots of evidence on that.

Knowledge@Wharton: What's an example?

Useem: Probably the best example that comes to mind very quickly here is what we learned from the United States Marine Corps. As we watch the officers and the officer candidate school train future Marine Corps officers, the teaching method is for people to get out, act, experience, succeed and fail, and then conduct what they call the "After Action Review." To take it apart—what went well? What did not go well? And that is, in my view, one of the great avenues for leadership development—which is to take apart your last day or your last week and reflect on it. After a couple years of doing those "after action reviews," you can say correctly with confidence, "My intuition tells me right now that we ought to be going in this direction and not that direction."

Knowledge@Wharton: So that's informed intuition?

Useem: Yes, informed intuition...informed by your own and other's experiences.

Knowledge@Wharton: So what is the biggest challenge that our leaders face today?

Useem: It's a really important question because it gets at whether leadership—and getting your leadership formula right—is really important. So here's the argument. For people in positions of responsibility organizationally, one of the best predictors of how much impact a given leader will have—a college president, a corporate manager, a country prime minister—is the extent to which the company, the university, or the country is facing changing or non-changing circumstances, and the extent to which the future is discernable and predictable or not. So, to make that more affirmative and to put it simply: If life looks like it's going to be more uncertain going ahead, you really want to get your leadership formula right. Think Greece as we speak, think companies in some of these tough telecom markets, think the globalization of firms now trying to get into the China or India market. If you're a leader of any of the above, you're facing, in the next five or 10 years, arguably more uncertain and more changing circumstances. If so, it's more critical than ever to get your leadership right. And what does it mean to get it right? You have to apply all 15 principles of the Leader's Checklist. One or five won't do it.

Knowledge@Wharton: What is the 16th principle?

Useem: The one that's not in there?

Knowledge@Wharton: The one that got away.

Useem: This is not meant to dodge your question, but I'm going to answer it in kind of a sideways fashion. As soon as you sit down and look at these 15, it's obvious. There is definitely no rocket science here. If you're going to lead, let's say as a mid-level manager at Google or at GE, you need a 16th and a 17th and an 18th principle, ones that apply to those particular settings. So in the case of GE, it's that unrelenting focus on getting results quarter in and quarter out. You just have to do it. You've got to be really good at that. At Google, it is sustaining intellectual energy and excitement about projects. I wouldn't make those universal, because at some organizations they are not vital. If you operate in India, it's going to be different ones than if you are operating in China. ■

© 2011 by Knowledge@Wharton. Adapted from the Knowledge@Wharton interview first published June 22, 2011.

Endnotes

[i] British Petroleum, *Deepwater Horizon: Accident Investigation Report*, September 8, 2010; National Commission on the BP Deepwater Horizon Oil Spill and Offshore Drilling, *Deep Water: The Gulf Oil Disaster and the Future of Offshore Drilling*, January 11, 2011; Michael Lewis, *The Big Short: Inside the Doomsday Machine*, Norton, 2011; Andrew Ross Sorkin, *Too Big to Fail: The Inside Story of How Wall Street and Washington Fought to Save the Financial System—and Themselves*, Viking Press, 2009; Bethany McLean and Joe Nocera, *All the Devils Are Here: The Hidden History of the Financial Crisis*, Portfolio, 2010.

[ii] Peter Elkind and Jennifer Reingold with Doris Burke, "Insider Pfizer's Palace Coup," *Fortune*, August 15, 2011.

[iii] Gerald F. Davis, *Managed by the Markets: How Finance Re-Shaped America*, Oxford University Press, 2009; Michael Useem, *Investor Capitalism: How Money Managers Are Changing the Face of Corporate America*, Basic Books/HarperCollins, 1996; Michael Useem, "Corporate Leadership in a Globalizing Equity Market," *Academy of Management Executive*, 12, 1998, pp. 43-59.

[iv] Michael Useem, "The Business of Employment: Time to Revise Investor Capitalism's Mantra," *Washington Post* On Leadership, August 9, 2011 (http://www.washingtonpost.com/national/on-leadership/the-business-of-employment-time-to-revise-investor-capitalisms-mantra/2011/08/09/gIQAh8rs4I_story.html).

ᵛ For a case on the rescue by Rodrigo Jordán, Matko Koljatic, and
Michael Useem, "Leading the Rescue of the Miners in Chile,"
Wharton School, Business Case, 2011 (http://kw.wharton.upenn.edu/
wdp/files/2011/07/Leading-the-Miners-Rescue.pdf). A special
exhibit on the rescue, "Against All Odds: Rescue at the Chilean
Mine," was opened by the Smithsonian Institution and the Embassy
of Chile at the National Museum of Natural History in Washington
in August, 2011 (http://www.si.edu/exhibitions/ details/Against-
All-Odds-Rescue-at-the-Chilean-Mine-4694). For an article that
more fully examines the leadership of Laurence Golborne, see
Michael Useem, Rodrigo Jordán, Matko Koljatic, "33 Below:
Learning Crisis Leadership from the Rescue of the Miners in Chile,"
MIT Sloan Management Review, Fall, 2011 (http://sloanreview.mit.edu/
the-magazine/2011-fall/53106/how-to-lead-during-a-crisis-lessons-
from-the-rescue-of-the-chilean-miners).

ᵛⁱ The film: *9/11: The Filmmakers' Commemorative Edition*, filmed
by Jules Naudet and Gedeon Naudet, directed by James Hanlon,
Jules Naudet, Rob Klug, 2002.

¹ Among the organizations are Abbott Laboratories, Accenture,
ADP, American Express, Amgen, Berkshire Partners, Canadian
Imperial Bank of Commerce, Cargill, CEO Academy, China
Minsheng Banking Corporation, Citigroup, Cisco Systems,
CITIC Bank (China), Coca-Cola, Columbia Energy, Comcast,
Computer Sciences Corporation, Daimler, Deloitte, DuPont,
Entergy, Eli Lilly, Estée Lauder Companies, Federal
Executive Institute, Fidelity Investments, GlaxoSmithKline,
Goldman Sachs, Google, Grupo Santander (Chile), Hartford
Insurance, Hearst, Hewlett-Packard, HSM, IBM, ICICI Bank
(India), Intel, Johnson & Johnson, Kimberly-Clark, KPMG,
Liberty Mutual Insurance, Lucent Technologies, MassMutual,
MasterCard, McGraw-Hill, Medtronic, Merck, Microsoft,
Milliken, Morgan Stanley, Motorola, the National Football
League, the New York City Fire Department, The New York
Times Company, Nokia, Northrop Grumman, Novartis, Penske,
Petrobras (Brazil), Petróleos de Venezuela, Pew Charitable Trusts,
PricewaterhouseCoopers, Progressive Insurance, Raytheon,
Samsung, Securities Association of China, Siemens, Singapore
General Hospital, Sprint, 3Com Corporation, Thomson Financial,
Toyota, Travelers, Verizon, United Healthcare, United Technologies,

the UN Development Programme, the U.S. Department of Justice, the U.S. Department of Veterans Affairs, the U.S. Marine Corps, the U.S. Military Academy, and the World Economic Forum. I have also annually worked on leadership development with 100 to 200 students enrolled in the Wharton Executive MBA program.

2 Albert Einstein, "On the Method of Theoretical Physics," *Philosophy of Science* 1 (1934): 163–69.

3 Michael Useem, *The Leadership Moment: Nine True Stories of Triumph and Disaster and Their Lessons for Us All* (New York: Random House, 1998), 142–143; Joseph Harder, "Louis Gerstner and Lotus Development," Business Case, Harvard Business School, 2000.

4 Howard Gardner with Emma Laskin, *Leading Minds: An Anatomy Of Leadership* (New York: Basic Books, 1996).

5 David F. Freedman, Corps Business: *The 30 Management Principles of the U.S. Marines* (New York: Harper Business, 1996); Michael Useem, "Four Lessons in Adaptive Leadership," *Harvard Business Review*, November 2010; "Lead Time," an interview with Warren Bennis, *World Link* magazine, January–February 1999.

6 Adam Bryant, "Never Duck the Tough Questions," *New York Times*, July 17, 2011; Adam Bryant, "Imagining a World of No Annual Reviews," *New York Times*, October 17, 2011. For leaders describing the capacities that have made the greatest difference to them, see Adam Bryant, *The Corner Office: Indispensible and Unexpected Lessons from CEOs on How to Lead and Succeed* (New York: Times Books, 2011); Mukul Pandya, Robbie Shell, and Nightly Business Report, *Lasting Leadership: What You Can Learn from the Top 25 Business People of Our Times* (Philadelphia: Wharton School Publishing and Boston: Pearson Education, 2004); Louis V. Gerstner Jr., *Who Says Elephants Can't Dance? How I Turned Around IBM* (New York: HarperCollins, 2003); Bill George, *Authentic Leadership: Rediscovering the Secrets to Creating Lasting Value* (Hoboken, NJ: Jossey-Bass, 2004); see also *The New York Times* "Corner Office" webpage, at http://projects.nytimes.com/corner-office, the *Wall Street Journal*'s

"Lessons in Leadership" webpage, at http://online.wsj.com/public/page/lessons-in-leadership.html?mod=WSJ_ topnav_na_ business, and the *Washington Post*'s "On Leadership" webpage, at http://www.washingtonpost.com/national/on-leadership.

[7] Peter Drucker, "Not Enough Generals Were Killed!" in *The Leader of the Future*, edited by Frances Hesselbein, Marshall Goldsmith, and Richard Beckhard (Hoboken, NJ: Jossey-Bass, 1996); Noel Tichy, *The Leadership Engine: How Winning Companies Build Leaders at Every Level* (New York: HarperCollins, 1997); Geoffrey Colvin, "How to Build Great Leaders," *Fortune*, November 20, 2009; Hewitt Associates, *Top Companies for Leaders*, Hewitt Associates, 2009.

[8] Frances Hesselbein, *My Life in Leadership: The Journey and Lessons Learned Along the Way* (Hoboken, NJ: Jossey-Bass, 2011); Daniel Goleman, "What Makes a Leader?" *Harvard Business Review*, November–December 1998, 93–102; Robert J. House, Paul J. Hanges, Mansour Javidan, Peter W. Dorfman, and Vipin Gupta, eds., *Culture, Leadership, and Organizations: The GLOBE Study of 62 Societies* (Thousand Oaks, CA: Sage Publications, 2004); Mansour Javidan, Peter W. Dorfman, Mary Sully de Luque, Robert J. House, "In the Eye of the Beholder: Cross Cultural Lessons in Leadership from Project GLOBE," *Academy of Management Perspectives* 20 (2006): 67–90. For examples of other academic assessments, see Nitin Nohria and Rakesh Khurana, eds., *Handbook of Leadership Theory and Practice* (Cambridge, MA: Harvard Business Press, 2010), and articles appearing in the *Leadership Quarterly*.

[9] Michael Useem, *Investor Capitalism: How Money Managers Are Changing the Face of Corporate America* (New York: Basic Books/HarperCollins, 1996); Michael Useem, "How Well-Run Boards Make Decisions," *Harvard Business Review*, November 2006, 130–38; Michael Useem and Andy Zelleke, "Oversight and Delegation in Corporate Governance: Deciding What the Board Should Decide," *Corporate Governance: An International Review* 14 (2006): 2–12; Michael Useem, "The Ascent of Shareholder Monitoring and Strategic Partnering: The Dual Functions of the Corporate Board," in *Sage Handbook on Corporate Governance*, edited by Thomas Clarke and Doug Branson (Thousand Oaks, CA: Sage Publications, 2012 [forthcoming]).

[10] Robert J. House, Paul J. Hanges, Mansour Javidan, Peter W. Dorfman, and Vipin Gupta, eds., *Culture, Leadership, and Organizations: The GLOBE Study of 62 Societies*, Sage Publications, 2004; Javidan et al., "In the Eye of the Beholder: Cross Cultural Lessons in Leadership from Project GLOBE," *Academy of Management Perspectives* 20 (2006): 67–90.

[11] Peter Cappelli, Harbir Singh, Jitendra Singh, and Michael Useem, *The India Way: How India's Top Business Leaders Are Revolutionizing Management* (Cambridge, MA: Harvard Business Press, 2010).

[12] John P. Kotter and Dan S. Cohen, *The Heart of Change: Real-Life Stories of How People Change Their Organizations* (Cambridge, MA: Harvard Business Press, 2002); see also David A. Nadler and Michael L. Tushman, "Beyond the Charismatic Leader: Leadership and Organizational Change," *California Management Review*, Winter 1990; Charles A. O'Reilly III and Michael L. Tushman, *Winning Through Innovation: A Practical Guide to Leading Organizational Change and Renewal* (Cambridge, MA: Harvard Business Press, 2002).

[13] Dennis Carey, Michael Patsalos-Fox, and Michael Useem, "Leadership Lessons for Hard Times," *McKinsey Quarterly*, July 2009.

[14] See, for instance, American Hospital Association, Measuring the Community Connection: A Strategy Checklist for Leaders, American Hospital Association, 2006 (http://www.caringfor-communities.org/ caringforcommunities/content/ strategy-checklist.pdf); William G. Bowen, *Lessons Learned: Reflections of a University President* (Princeton, NJ: Princeton University Press, 2010); Jim Collins, *Good to Great and the Social Sectors* (New York: HarperCollins, 2005); Marshall Ganz, *Why David Sometimes Wins: Leadership, Organization, and Strategy in the California Farm Worker Movement* (New York: Oxford University Press, 2010); John W. Gardner, *On Leadership* (New York: Free Press, 1993); General Accounting Office, *Human Capital: A Self-Assessment Checklist for Agency Leaders*, 1999; David Gergen, *Eyewitness to Power: The Essence of Leadership from Nixon to Clinton* (New York: Simon & Schuster, 2001); Mel Gill, Robert J.

Flynn, and Elke Reissing, "The Governance Self-Assessment
Checklist: An Instrument for Assessing Board Effectiveness,"
Nonprofit Management and Leadership 15 (2005): 271–94; Doris
Kearns Goodwin, *Team of Rivals: The Political Genius of Abraham
Lincoln* (New York: Simon & Schuster, 2005); Nannerl O.
Keohane, *Higher Ground: Ethics and Leadership in the Modern University*
(Durham, NC: Duke University Press, 2006); Mike Krzyzewski
and Donald T. Phillips, *Leading with the Heart: Coach K's
Successful Strategies for Basketball, Business, and Life* (New York:
Business Plus/Hachette, 2001); Pat Summit, *Reach for the
Summit* (New York: Broadway Books, 1999); D. Michael Lindsay,
*Faith in the Halls of Power: How Evangelicals Joined the American
Elite* (New York: Oxford University Press, 2008); Joe Torre and
Henry Dreher, *Joe Torre's Ground Rules for Winners: 12 Keys to
Managing Team Players, Tough Bosses, Setbacks, and Success*
(New York: Hyperion, 2000); Barbara Turnbull, "Evaluating
School-Based Management: A Tool for Team Self-Review,"
International Journal of Leadership in Education 8 (2005): 73–79;
John Wooden and Steve Jamison, *Wooden on Leadership: How to
Create a Winning Organization* (New York: McGraw-Hill, 2005);
"Filling in the 'Missing Pieces': How Mary Ellen Iskenderian
and Women's World Banking Are Redefining Microfinance,"
Knowledge@Wharton, July 7, 2010 (http://knowledge.wharton.
upenn.edu/article.cfm?articleid=2540).

[15] John Baldoni, *Lead Your Boss: The Subtle Art of Managing Up*
(New York: Amacom, 2009); John J. Gabarro and John P. Kotter,
"Managing Your Boss," *Harvard Business Review*, January 2005;
Michael Useem, *Leading Up: How to Lead Your Boss So You Both
Win* (New York: Crown Business/Random House, 2002).

[16] Samuel Linn, Alpha Company, 52nd Infantry Regiment (AT),
5/2 Stryker Brigade Combat Team, U.S. Army, Kandahar,
Afghanistan, 2009–2010, personal communication, February
8–9; Center for Army Lessons Learned, http://usacac.army.mil/
cac2/call/index.asp (not open to the public).

[17] National Interagency Fire Center, *Incident Response Pocket
Guide*, http://www.nwcg.gov/pms/pubs/pubs.htm, January 2010,
and also available as an iPad app, iRPG; New York City Fire
Department, Chief Officer Operational Checklists, November
16, 2005.

[18] Pre-Sales Checklist prepared by Ralf Klein and John Gobron, Microsoft, 2010, personal communication.

[19] Bryant, "Google's Quest to Build a Better Boss."

[20] Michael Useem, Michael Barriere, and Joseph Ryan, "Looking South to See North: Upward Appraisal of Tangible Leadership," Wharton Center for Leadership and Change, University of Pennsylvania, 2011.

[21] Atul Gawande, *The Checklist Manifesto: How to Get Things Right* (New York: Holt, 2009); Alex B. Haynes et. al., "A Surgical Safety Checklist to Reduce Morbidity and Mortality in a Global Population," *New England Journal of Medicine* 360 (2009): 491–99; John D. Brinkmeyer, "Strategies for Improving Surgical Quality—Checklists and Beyond," *New England Journal of Medicine* 363 (2010): 1963–65; Eefje N. de Vries et al., "Effect of a Comprehensive Surgical Safety System on Patient Outcomes," *New England Journal of Medicine* 363 (2010): 1928–37.

[22] Jeffrey Pfeffer and Robert I. Sutton, *The Knowing-Doing Gap: How Smart Companies Turn Knowledge Into Action* (Cambridge, MA: Harvard Business School Press, 2000).

[23] Norman Maclean, *Young Men and Fire* (Chicago: University of Chicago Press, 1993); Useem, *The Leadership Moment*, 1998; Michael Useem; "In the Heat of the Moment: A Case Study in Life-and-Death Decision Making," *Fortune*, June 27, 2005: 125–33.

[24] The account that follows draws on Useem, *The Leadership Moment* (and a number of sources cited therein), and Roy Vagelos and Louis Galambos, Medicine, Science, and Merck (Cambridge, MA: Cambridge University Press, 2004).

[25] Michael Useem, *The Go Point: When It's Time to Decide* (New York: Random House, 2006), 214.

[26] Michael Useem, "John Chambers: Whether Up or Down, Always Innovating," *U.S. News & World Report*, November 2009; the phrase "touching the void" is borrowed from Joe Simpson's *Touching the Void: The True Story of One Man's Miraculous Survival* (New York: Perennial, 2004).

[27] We draw upon several sources, including American International Group, Inc., 2008 *Annual Report*; Roddy Boyd, *Fatal Risk: A Cautionary Tale of AIG's Corporate Suicide* (Hoboken, NJ: Wiley, 2011); Eric Dickinson, "Credit Default Swaps: So Dear to Us, So Dangerous," *Fordham Law School*, November 20, 2008; Eric Dinallo, Testimony to the U.S. Senate Committee on Banking, Housing and Urban Affairs, March 5, 2009; Donald L. Kohn, Statement to the U.S. Senate Committee on Banking, Housing, and Urban Affairs, March 5, 2009; Ben Levisohn, "AIG's CDS Hoard: The Great Unraveling," *Business Week Online*, April 7, 2009; Steve Lohr, "In Modeling Risk, the Human Factor Was Left Out," *New York Times*, November 5, 2008; Nell Minow, Testimony to the U.S. House of Representatives Committee on Oversight and Government Reform, October 7, 2008; Carrick Mollenkamp, Serena Ng, Liam Pleven, and Randall Smith, "Behind AIG's Fall, Risk Models Failed to Pass Real-World Test," *Wall Street Journal*, October 31, 2008; Gretchen Morgenson, "Behind Insurer's Crisis, Blind Eye to a Web of Risk," *New York Times*, September 28, 2008; Scott M. Polakoff, Statement to the U.S. Senate Committee on Banking, House and Urban Affairs, March 5, 2009; William K. Sjostrom, Jr., "The AIG Bailout," Salmon P. Chase School of Law, Northern Kentucky University, March 10, 2009; and Gillian Tett, *Fool's Gold: How Unrestrained Greed Corrupted a Dream, Shattered Markets, and Unleashed a Catastrophe* (New York: Little, Brown, 2009).

[28] Morgenson, "Behind Insurer's Crisis, Blind Eye to a Web of Risk."

[29] Levisohn, "AIG's CDS Hoard: The Great Unraveling."

[30] Morgenson, "Behind Insurer's Crisis, Blind Eye to a Web of Risk"; Minow, Testimony to the U.S. House of Representatives Committee on Oversight and Government Reform, 2008.

[31] Polakoff, Statement to the U.S. Senate Committee on Banking, House and Urban Affairs, 2009.

[32] Itshak Ben-David, John R. Graham, and Campbell R. Harvey, "Managerial Overconfidence and Corporate Policies," Duke University, 2007; Anand M. Goel and Anjan V. Thakor, "Over-

confidence, CEO Selection, and Corporate Governance,"
Journal of Finance 63 (2008): 2737–84; Haim Mano, "Risk-
Taking, Framing Effects, and Affect," *Organizational Behavior
and Human Decision Processes* 57 (1994): 38–58; William F.
Wright, "Mood Effects on Subjective Probability Assessment,"
Organizational Behavior and Human Decision Processes 52
(1992): 276–91.

[33] Useem, *The Leadership Moment*; for useful illustrations of
learning leadership from leaders' failures, not just exemplary
behavior, see "The Failure Issue: How to Understand It, Learn
from It, and Recover from It," *Harvard Business Review*, April
2011; Sydney Finkelstein, *Why Smart Executives Fail and What
You Can Learn from Their Mistakes*, (New York: Portfolio, 2003);
Tim Irwin, *Derailed: Five Lessons Learned from Catastrophic
Failures of Leadership* (New York: Thomas Nelson, 2009);
Robert E. Mittelstaedt Jr., *Will Your Next Mistake Be Fatal?
Avoiding the Chain of Mistakes That Can Destroy Your Organization*
(New York: Pearson, 2004); Jeffrey Sonnenfeld and Andrew
Ward, *Firing Back: How Great Leaders Rebound from Career
Decisions* (Cambridge, MA: Harvard Business Press, 2007).

[34] Jonathan Franklin, *33 Men: Inside the Miraculous Survival and
Dramatic Rescue of the Chilean Miners* (New York: Putnam,
2011); Rodrigo Jordán, Matko Koljatic, and Michael Useem,
"Leading the Rescue of the Miners in Chile," Wharton School,
Business Case, 2011; Michael Useem, Rodrigo Jordán, and
Matko Koljatic, "33 Below: Learning Crisis Leadership and
General Management from the Rescue of the Miners in Chile,"
Wharton Center for Leadership, University of Pennsylvania, 2011.

[35] The narrative and direct quotes are from sources cited in the
prior endnote. In preparing those articles, we have drawn upon
extensive media coverage of the rescue and personal interviews
with the leader of the rescue and the members of the top rescue
team: René Aguilar, head of safety, El Teniente mine, Codelco
(National Copper Corporation of Chile), and deputy chief on
rescue site, December 22, 2010; Cristián Barra, cabinet chief,
Ministry of the Interior, Republic of Chile, January 5, 2010;
Laurence Golborne, mining minister, Republic of Chile,
November 1, 2010; Luz Granier, chief of staff to the mining

minister, November 1, 2010; and André Sougarret, manager, El Teniente mine, Codelco, and chief engineer on rescue site, January 5, 2010.

[36] D. A. Waldman, G. G. Ramirez, R. J. House, and P. Puranan, "Does Leadership Matter: CEO Leadership Attributes and Profitability Under Conditions of Perceived Environmental Uncertainty," *Academy of Management Journal* 44 (2001); 134–43; Alan Berkeley Thomas, "Does Leadership Make a Difference to Organizational Performance?" *Administrative Science Quarterly* 33 (1988): 388–400; Stanley Lieberson and James F. O'Connor, "Leadership and Organizational Performance: A Study of Large Corporations," *American Sociological Review* 37 (1972): 117–30.

[37] Adam Goodheart, *1861: The Civil War Awakening* (New York: Knopf, 2011); Drew Gilpin Faust, *This Republic of Suffering: Death and the American Civil War* (New York: Knopf, 2008).

[38] Joshua Lawrence Chamberlain, *Passing of the Armies: The Last Campaign of the Armies* (Gettysburg, PA: Stan Clark Military Books, 1994), 261.

[39] Chamberlain, *Passing of the Armies*; Douglas Southall Freeman, *Lee's Lieutenants: A Study in Command,* abridged in one volume by Stephen W. Sears (New York: Scribners, 1998); William Marvel, *Lee's Last Retreat: The Flight to Appomattox* (Durham, NC: University of North Carolina Press, 2002); Alice Rains Trulock, *In the Hands of Providence: Joshua L. Chamberlain and the American Civil War* (Durham, NC: University of North Carolina Press, 1992); Jay Winik, *April 1865: The Month That Saved America* (New York: HarperCollins, 2001).

[40] Jim Collins, *Good to Great: Why Some Companies Make the Leap...and Others Don't* (New York: HarperBusiness, 2001).

[41] Helene Cooper, "Medal of Honor for Bravery in Afghanistan," *New York Times,* November 16, 2011; also see http://www.army. mil/medalofhonor/giunta/citation.html and http://www.youtube.com/watch?v= R2RWscJM97U

About the Author

MICHAEL USEEM is director of the Center for Leadership and Change Management and William and Jacalyn Egan Professor of Management at The Wharton School of the University of Pennsylvania. He is the author of *The Leadership Moment, Investor Capitalism,* and *The Go Point,* among other books. *The Leadership Moment* was included in *The 100 Best Business Books of All Time,* written by the publishers of *800-CEO-READ,* and it was listed as one of the ten best leadership books on the *Washington Post*'s "Leadership Playlist." Useem's articles have appeared in the *Chicago Tribune, Fast Company, Financial Times, Fortune, Harvard Business Review, McKinsey Quarterly, The New York Times, U.S. News & World Report,* the *Washington Post,* the *Wall Street Journal,* and elsewhere.

Useem has presented programs and seminars on leadership development with American Express, China Minsheng Banking Corporation, Citigroup, Coca-Cola, Comcast, Eli Lilly, Estée Lauder, Fidelity Investments, GlaxoSmithKline, Goldman Sachs, Google, Grupo Santander, Hewlett-Packard, Intel, Johnson & Johnson, Microsoft, Morgan Stanley, Motorola, the National Football League, the New York City Fire Department, The New York Times Company, Nokia,

Pew Charitable Trusts, PricewaterhouseCoopers, Samsung, the UN Development Programme, the U.S. Department of Justice, the U.S. Department of Veterans Affairs, the U.S. Marine Corps, the U.S. Military Academy, the World Economic Forum, and other organizations. ∎

About Wharton Digital Press

Wharton Digital Press was established to inspire bold, insightful thinking within the global business community. In the tradition of The Wharton School of the University of Pennsylvania and its online business journal *Knowledge @Wharton*, Wharton Digital Press uses innovative digital technologies to help managers meet the challenges of today and tomorrow.

As an entrepreneurial publisher, Wharton Digital Press delivers relevant, accessible, conceptually sound, and empirically based business knowledge to readers wherever and whenever they need it. Its format ranges from ebooks and enhanced ebooks to mobile apps and print books available through print-on-demand technology. Directed to a general business audience, the Press's areas of interest include management and strategy, innovation and entrepreneurship, finance and investment, leadership, marketing, operations, human resources, social responsibility, business-government relations, and more.

http://wdp.wharton.upenn.edu

About The Wharton School

The Wharton School of the University of Pennsylvania—founded in 1881 as the first collegiate business school—is recognized globally for intellectual leadership and ongoing innovation across every major discipline of business education. The most comprehensive source of business knowledge in the world, Wharton bridges research and practice through its broad engagement with the global business community. The School has more than 4,800 undergraduate, MBA, executive MBA, and doctoral students; more than 9,000 annual participants in executive education programs; and an alumni network of 86,000 graduates.

http://www.wharton.upenn.edu

CPSIA information can be obtained at www.ICGtesting.com
Printed in the USA
BVOW021126260212

283837BV00003B/56/P